Under Construction

Under Construction

BECAUSE LIVING MY BEST LIFE TOOK A LITTLE WORK

CHRISHELL STAUSE

WITH DINA GACHMAN

GALLERY BOOKS

NEW YORK   LONDON   TORONTO   SYDNEY   NEW DELHI

G

Gallery Books
An Imprint of Simon & Schuster, Inc.
1230 Avenue of the Americas
New York, NY 10020

First Gallery Books hardcover edition February 2022

GALLERY BOOKS and colophon are registered trademarks
of Simon & Schuster, Inc.

For information about special discounts for bulk purchases,
please contact Simon & Schuster Special Sales at 1-866-506-1949
or business@simonandschuster.com.

The Simon & Schuster Speakers Bureau can bring authors to your live event.
For more information or to book an event, contact the Simon & Schuster Speakers
Bureau at 1-866-248-3049 or visit our website at www.simonspeakers.com.

Interior design by Michelle Marchese

Manufactured in the United States of America

1   3   5   7   9   10   8   6   4   2

Library of Congress Cataloging-in-Publication Data has been applied for.

ISBN 978-1-9821-8625-8
ISBN 978-1-9821-8627-2 (ebook)

This book is dedicated to the person
who planted the fire in my soul
and the kindness in my heart.
I miss you every day, Mom.

Contents

CHAPTER ONE

Suck It Up, Buttercup

Sitting down to write this feels surreal. A publisher wants *me* to write a book? I have never been so flattered and terrified at the same time—and this is coming from someone who was asked to dress as Cinderella and dance the waltz on live TV, in front of millions of people. That experience had nothing on the experience of putting my life down on paper, for anyone to read. I have always loved writing and can remember several times being the kid whose paper was picked to be read aloud, which did wonders for my "cool" points in school. I have often used writing as an outlet after heartbreak, putting my thoughts and feelings down in those have-to-remember-this life moments. But the thought of *other people* reading your deepest thoughts creates a lot of pressure. That said, I'm grateful you're here, and I'm guessing that if you are reading this (so sweet, I love you for life, thank you!), then you know a bit about me already. If you don't know much about me, I'd say I'm a determined, ambitious dreamer who leads with her heart. I'm also a Realtor, a soap actor, and one of the stars of *Selling Sunset*, the Netflix show about luxury Realtors in Los Angeles. A lot has been written about my life over the years, and many times it's coming from "anonymous sources," but everything in the pages of this book is coming straight from one source—me.

You may have seen me on top of the world, and also knocked on my ass more than once. I don't claim to have the key to success, but I can tell you what's worked for me. Life so far has been filled with struggle and adversity, triumphs and victories. I haven't figured out how to stay on top, but I have figured out how to get back there after a fall or two. I've learned to be down, but not out. Throughout the years, I have found ways to be mentally strong so I can get up, dress up, and show up in those pivotal moments where it's all too tempting to want to melt into the ground and disappear. I am obviously still a work in progress, and just like any great construction project, sometimes you have to knock down a few walls to let in the light. Every remodel begins with a mess, and I'm certainly no exception.

When I look at my life now, I'm surrounded by mansions, millionaires, celebrities, and red carpets. A far cry from where it all began. The farthest cry. How far can a cry actually go? Okay, you get the point. But sometimes people see my dresses, stiletto heels, and carefully applied lashes and assume I'd be as out of place roughing it as *Sex and the City*'s Manhattan-loving Carrie Bradshaw every time Aidan took her to his cabin in the woods. I used to secretly enjoy it when people in Los Angeles and New York mistook me for a high-maintenance girl who wouldn't last five minutes on a camping trip. If they only knew. But the fact that they didn't meant I had successfully blended into my new city life, and my dirty little secret was still safe.

When people mistook me for a "Carrie," I'd contemplate confessing that I actually missed a whole year of middle school due to our house burning down, forcing us to live in a tent, hopping from campsite to campsite. Sure, it was tempting to shock them with tips for finding the best spot to put up your tent (soft ground, but not wet; higher is better) or washing your hair in a river or lake (downstream is God's water pressure, not to mention that you might forget about your chigger and mosquito bites for a short, heavenly reprieve). But instead of correcting people, I almost felt victorious that I had fooled them into thinking I actually belonged to the life I was living. One that entailed going to red carpet events with grand titles like galas and premieres and living out my dream of becoming the most glamorous thing I could think of as a kid: a soap star.

Even though I feel like I successfully manifested this life (and by manifested, I mean hustled my ass off), in no way did it come easy.

I remember having to work to keep a straight face when asked if I competed in beauty pageants growing up in the South. Me? The awkward brown-haired girl with the mustache and the rogue tooth? The one who worked at Dairy Queen in high school and dreamed of one day being on a billboard or in a magazine, despite those beauty roadblocks? And despite how people may perceive me, in many ways I'm still the scrappy kid born in Chaffee, Missouri, whose hospital I was born in isn't even there anymore. If you've never heard of the town, you're not alone.

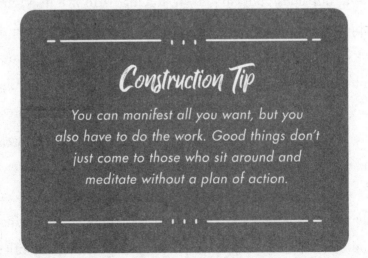

Construction Tip

You can manifest all you want, but you also have to do the work. Good things don't just come to those who sit around and meditate without a plan of action.

I love and adore my family and would do absolutely anything for them, but I'm embarrassed to admit that I felt ashamed of them for many years. It was a long journey of me slowly finding myself and shaking my own self-doubt and insecurities before I could finally own where I came from and speak about it. For many years a big part of me feared judgment, like I would never be accepted because I would forever be associated with a life I had tried so hard to deny and get away from. Even in the process of looking back at myself in photos for this book, it was surprising not to see a Shrek-like monster looking back at me. It's funny how insecurities completely change your perception of yourself. Because now when I look at photos of that time, I just see a regular little girl. She didn't need to be self-conscious simply because she was walking or talking or breathing. She didn't need to shrink and hide. I wish I could tell her, *Your mustache isn't even that noticeable!* I would also love to just tell her to pluck it while I'm at it! It took me way too long to figure that out. All it takes is one kid teasing you about a mustache one time in life to hit a nerve, and then that is what you are teased about for years to come. You never forget those moments, but hopefully you can one day look back and realize that it wasn't all that bad, and that the person being the bully is the one who truly needs the help. I actually developed quite the retort for the times kids (I see you, Greg Chasen) would make fun of my mustache. I would say, "At least I have hair somewhere, where it counts." The laughter of the other kids meant that I had just bought myself a little time to be left alone.

It wasn't just my five o'clock shadow (which I was terrified of removing because I was scared it would grow back darker) that wrecked my confidence. It also didn't help that sometimes I was one of the kids who didn't make it back to class after a head lice check, or that I was on a free lunch program that meant you had to show a card at lunchtime that was *a different color card* from all the other kids' cards. Those things are mortifying at that age. To avoid embarrassment I would either hang back and go last in line, or skip lunch altogether. My parents also chain-smoked cigarettes in the house and used kerosene for heat (it was cheaper), which made our clothes smell all day long. While other girls smelled like Love's Baby Soft or Debbie Gibson's Electric Youth scent, I smelled like an old ashtray. Not fun. And then there was the time I made the color guard dance and music team, but then I had to quit once my family saw the expenses for band camp. Not that band camp would have launched me to instant popularity, but it was something. I also couldn't possibly admit why I was quitting, and in trying to pretend I had just changed my mind after a long audition process, I ended up with a few enemies. Imagine the girls patiently helping me learn the routine, and then I make the team, only to pretend I didn't want to do it anymore. They were pissed, and rightly so. I wish I had had the courage to be honest back then, but somehow it seemed the lesser of two evils, so I stayed quiet.

I went by my first name then. My full name is Terrina Chrishell Stause. I hated every single thing about myself in high school, including my name. I once asked my mom why she picked Terrina, and she just said she liked it because she had never heard it before. She had a flair for unique names, which you can tell by the names of our German shepherds growing up: Nakia (Na-KIGH-a), Tisha, and Trippy. Trippy got his name because he was shaken as a puppy and he lost his equilibrium, which made him trip everywhere, but they were also 1970s hippies so I'm sure his name was also inspired by a few recreational activities. We also had cats named Kiara and Chakita, and a racoon named Bandit. So as much as I wanted to blend in growing up and have a name like Sarah or Jennifer, it wasn't in the cards for me. I would later grow to really love my unique name, but we have a ways to go before that part of the story.

A few crazy stories are swirling around online about how my mom came up with my middle name, Chrishell. Despite what you may or may not have read, I was not born at a Shell gas station. That story has grown legs and multiplied over the years, but really my mom was having car trouble and she pulled into a Shell station. She went into labor while she was waiting on the car, and the gas station attendant was very sweet and calm, and he made sure my mom got to a hospital so that I wouldn't enter this world next to a gas pump (and probably so he wouldn't have to deliver a baby). His kindness inspired my mom to name me after the attendant, Chris, and so Chrishell was born, literally. My dad used to joke that it was a good thing I wasn't born at a Texaco. I would have been Chrisexico.

When I went off to college it was time for me to shed my life as Terrina and start over. I had all new classmates who didn't know my secrets. They didn't know about the campgrounds or the ashtray smell or the struggles. They had no clue we were on food stamps and that I sometimes slept in an attic. As soon as I started going by Chrishell, it was the beginning of being able to embrace my personality and be myself—without giving up my past. I told my two best friends, Elly and Julie, whom I'm still close with to this day, but otherwise it just didn't come up that much. I was constantly working and going to class, so besides work and exams, college conversations were usually about where we were going to go out that night. I did have one college boyfriend who broke up with me as soon as he came home to meet my family and saw their trailer. I think he saw me as "different" after that, and not as the type of girl who would have been acceptable to bring home to a no doubt beautiful estate. So because of those experiences, I felt like I had to hide where I really came from. Now that I've found success and become established it doesn't seem to bring on as much judgment. In fact, the opposite. It's become something I can be proud of. But back then, it really felt like it tainted how some people saw me. So I kept it to myself and focused on my goals.

It wasn't as if my childhood was *The Hunger Games*, where I had to take up arms and fight for my life (well, not quite). My parents did the best they could, and in hindsight I'm thankful that I grew up learning how to be resilient and resourceful. My parents were freedom-loving hippies at heart. They once came to a Halloween party when they were visiting me in college and people thought their actual clothes were hippie costumes. Yes, they had their struggles with addiction and mental illness, and yes, I've forgiven them for those years they thought it was a good idea to join the Worldwide Church of God. *Legally* I can't say it was a cult, but it sure *felt* like a cult, because they forbade members from celebrating birthdays and Christmas, and they would randomly make house calls to make sure you were still earning your way to heaven. Despite all of that, I focus on the positive lessons I learned from them. And there are too many to count. My parents might not have been the best at remembering to pick me up from my plays or ever making a track meet. They didn't understand the point of running in a circle (and upon reflection, it's a pretty valid argument), but I have no doubt that needing to be resourceful and street-smart at an early age was instrumental in getting me to where I am now. I learned to be very adaptable, and that helped me when auditioning for roles and needing to pretend to be someone else. It also helped me realize that the cult's "gospel" was only based on the Old Testament. I remember telling my mom, "There's a sequel called the New Testament, you need to read it." My parents got into the cult when I was about ten years old. Reader, if you go to a church and you have a "leader," instead of a pastor or rabbi or minister, that's your first clue that this might be a cult. When we moved to Kentucky a few years after they joined, we didn't have a chapter anywhere near our small town. The leader died and his son took over and drastically changed some beliefs, so my parents ended up walking away. Thankfully that ended my extra homework of Bible quizzes and weekly check-ins from church elders.

All these life experiences ironically came in handy later on, even when selling multimillion-dollar homes to Los Angeles's elite, or needing to find my place in reality TV among one of the toughest social circles this side of 90210. I didn't go through life with a sense of "I deserve this." I've gone through it with a determination that no matter what, I would never end up washing my hair in a river again. There is also something very freeing about having nothing, so in turn having nothing to lose, and everything to gain.

Whatever your background is, it's key to remember that no matter what life hands you, you have to suck it up, believe in your abilities, and go after your wildest dreams, regardless of what the haters say. It's not always easy, and just like everyone else, I definitely have moments of doubt and fear and second guesses. I'm still that little girl from Chaffee with a rogue tooth. But I can always conjure up the sight of my house burning down or the feeling of clocking into a service job after school and know that I got this. If I survived all that, I can get through pretty much anything.

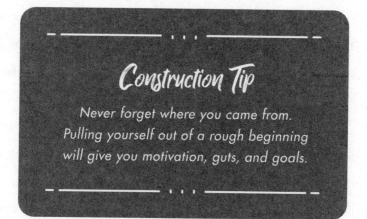

Construction Tip

Never forget where you came from.
Pulling yourself out of a rough beginning
will give you motivation, guts, and goals.

You don't have to have lived the kind of childhood I lived to be resilient or successful, but believing you can do something despite what everyone around you might think is definitely a major motivator. It kind of comes down to knowing who you are at your core, not forgetting that, and not letting anyone—not bosses, strangers, or colleagues, no matter how intimidating their power ponytails might be—derail you from your dreams.

Despite all odds, my earliest dream actually did come true.

As a little girl, I clearly remember my mom and grandmother watching their favorite soap operas, or their "stories," as they called them, on TV. Yes, growing up, there were times when we did have a house, and we had a TV, which was my dad's prized possession. (Mine was a New Kids on the Block poster that may as well have been a shrine.) When we didn't have our own home or TV, we'd watch at a friend's or relative's place, like my grandmother's house, or my dad's old boss Lonnie Roberts's place. Mr. Roberts let us live in his house in Draffenville, Kentucky, for two years when I was in high school. In my memory that house was absolutely beautiful, even though it was probably just a simple house with central AC, a solid roof, and no fleas or pests. It was basically my dream home at the time. For my sisters and me, living in a regular house, as simple as it probably was, was the height of the good life. I would love to go back to those houses now and see how they hold up to my memories. Something tells me they'd seem way less grand than I once thought they were. At that point in life, I had no concept of six-thousand-square-foot hillside homes in Hollywood with Olympic-size pools, chef's kitchens, and thirteen-foot ceilings. As a kid, if the ceilings didn't have gaping holes in them, I was sold.

My mom and dad were a far cry from stage parents who give up their jobs, move to Hollywood, and manage their kids' careers. My biological dad was half Japanese and half Spanish, but he and my mom broke up before she even knew she was pregnant. My mom was in love with my lifelong dad, Jeff, when she realized she was pregnant with my biological dad's baby. *What in the Tom Brady?* So my dad Jeff adopted me at birth and raised me as his own until we lost him to cancer a few years ago. He worked as a mechanic on and off, and his real dream was to be a drummer in a rock band. He drummed in several different cover bands his whole life because it was his passion. No, he never ended up opening for Led Zeppelin, but it made him so happy that he mostly drummed in exchange for gas money and beer. Some of my favorite memories are of watching him play and do his signature drumstick spin. He was self-taught and incredibly talented. When my dad and his friends did play a gig, my job was to dismantle the drum set and pack it up. I loved doing it. I was definitely not old enough to be there, but it made me feel important. So no, he wasn't a stage parent. He was actually on the stage playing drums and bringing me along as his roadie.

My mom had odd jobs here and there throughout her life, but nothing steady. For a while she worked as a caretaker for an elderly man named Mr. Harmon, and I bonded with him because we both loved books and reading. Then there was the job cleaning medical office buildings at night. She would have me go with her to help out, and I would always take the pharmaceutical-branded pens and Post-it notes out of the trash can to keep for myself. One doctor's trash was my treasure, I guess. A brand-new pen hocking allergy medicine? Sure! Post-it notes in a pill-shaped dispenser? Hell yes! Searching for these discarded gems helped me pass the time while we cleaned.

Most memorably, my mom worked at Dairy Queen with me *as her boss*. If memory serves, she lasted two weeks, and that might even be generous. My mother was a free-spirited, no-one-can-tell-me-what-to-do kind of badass. She thought all the Dairy Queen employee rules were dumb and that they either didn't matter or that she knew better than whoever made them up. One day during her brief stint, I walked up to find her working the drive-through window while SMOKING, but more on that later. My mom is a legend.

She truly embodied the IDGAF spirit, and I'll always love that about her, even if it made some of her decisions questionable, to say the least.

When I wasn't snagging Viagra pens out of the trash or filling cups at Dairy Queen, I spent much of my early years reading like a maniac. Soaps and books opened my mind up and showed me an entirely different world that was out there, waiting for me. This was before the internet, which makes me sound old, but "back then" we learned about the world from books, movies, or TV. I could not get enough of those "choose your own adventure" books, which kind of makes sense since I left my small town as soon as I could in search of adventure. While other kids were complaining about our reading assignments in school, I was devouring some of them two or three times. Reader, this is not me bragging about my literary skills. I was an unpopular kid without much of a social circle, so instead of spending the day at the local pool I would be in my room reading *Wuthering Heights*, *Romeo and Juliet*, and *Jane Eyre*. I guess those appealed to the future hopeless romantic in me. I also devoured *The Odyssey* (maybe hinting at a love of travel?), *The Canterbury Tales* (also about a journey), *The Count of Monte Cristo*, and *Great Expectations* (just great storytelling). Watching *Guiding Light* and *The Young and the Restless* with my mom and grandmother introduced me to the glamour of the daytime soap world. I knew from a young age that the life I was living was not the life I was *going* to live. There was something else out there for me, waiting. I was completely driven by that thought. I knew it in my bones.

But then there was that mustache. I was so embarrassed about it, and no one ever told me I could wax it or pluck it, so I got bullied in school. And let me tell you, there were no boyfriends anywhere in sight. Add to that the crooked teeth and my thrift store clothes—which definitely once belonged to the other kids in school in my small town—and you don't exactly get an image that screams *destined for the Daytime Emmys*. Still, somehow I just knew deep down that I'd leave that place, make something of myself, and get out of those clothes. The mustache? It took me a while before I learned how to take care of that mess. I don't remember asking my mom about it, but if I did she probably would have said something like, "You're beautiful the way you are, and screw anyone who doesn't think so!" She didn't give me beauty tips, but she did give me a certain fiery, "I can do this and move out of the way if you don't believe me" attitude that has helped me reach goals and keep moving forward, despite the odds. So, thank you, Mom. The legacy she left in the hearts she touched is still very present.

Construction Tip

Sometimes the best beauty advice is what my mom would say every time I got worked up about something: "Go outside and play."

Growing up the way we did, my siblings and I never had friends over. Was I going to invite them to our minuscule trailer? Or to a campground? At age eleven, I remember watching our house burn down. No one was hurt, but the little we had was lost. That started our campground hopping, and we were pulled out of school. I was miserable. Not exactly the type of place to have friends over, if I had friends to invite. At this point, I've lost count of how many times I moved as a kid.

For a short time I moved in with my grandmother (under the condition that she kick her creepy boyfriend out) in West Plains, Missouri. I suddenly realized a perk of your house burning down is that you needed to get all new clothes. When I started school there and for the first time lived in a house suitable to have friends over for sleepovers, they thought I was a "rich kid." It was the coolest thing that had ever happened to me, and I never once corrected them. Kind of like how for so long I didn't correct people who assumed I've always had access to million-dollar homes or designer bags. Maybe that was one of my early attempts at acting, just going along with this role of the girl who lives in a nice house with new clothes and shoes, a role I so desperately wanted. The role was short-lived once I went back to live with my parents, but my dream was still growing bigger.

I was determined to be on TV, so when one of our houses made the news by being the scene of a drive-by shooting, I saw an opportunity. Definitely not the typical path of a pageant queen. At the time we lived in a duplex, and this was the moment I learned we were sharing a wall with our nice neighbor who was a drug dealer. Apparently a deal went wrong, but luckily no one was home at the time of the shooting. I will never forget being so excited to see a news crew in our driveway the next morning. I remember running out to ambush newscaster Amy Watson, who was our local celebrity, to see if she would let me shadow her for a day. I think it worked to my advantage that she couldn't really say no considering we were both looking at a gunshot right below my bedroom window, which was technically an attic window. If anything, I am an opportunist.

When the day came to meet Amy for my faux day as a newscaster, we all met in the studio at five a.m. for the daily company rundown. Here I was, a high school student sitting among professionals, producers, and on-air talent. I was in heaven. On this day I would learn that being an anchor entailed much more than just getting your hair and makeup done and reading the news on camera. That day I watched Amy travel to places they would be covering, interview people on and off camera, write her own copy, and even help edit the piece—all with stressful deadlines looming. The whole day was so hectic I ended up feeling like I had been spit out of a tornado. Then to top it all off, when it was finally time to read the news on camera, there was Amy, doing her own makeup. My takeaways from that day were that newscasters in smaller markets absolutely need a pay raise, they get way too little credit for the work they actually do, and that Amy Watson is a national treasure.

As you can probably guess by now, a career in acting didn't fall into my lap. Sophomore year of high school I auditioned to play Dorothy in *The Wizard of Oz* at school, but I became disheartened when I was cast as Toto. You know, Dorothy's *dog*. This was not a thespian pressure cooker, like Beverly Hills High or a performing arts school in Manhattan. It was a small school in Draffenville, Kentucky, with a tiny theater department, and I got cast as a dog with no lines. Even the talking trees that threw apples at Dorothy were speaking. I was humiliated. Of course I got the speech from one of the teachers that there were no small roles, only small actors. But what did that speech mean to a high school kid who would have to give up several hours at her job managing the town Dairy Queen to play the dog with no lines? It meant I never actually played Toto, and I showed up at DQ in my red polo every day after school instead. I had to make a choice, and I guess I chose my paycheck over, yes, a very small part. No offense to all the actors who got their start playing Toto.

But things started to look up the next year when I tried again and finally landed the lead in the high school play! What was my breakout role, you might ask? Was it Cinderella in *Into the Woods*, or maybe Emily in *Our Town*? Nope. I played Mowgli from *The Jungle Book*. You know, the prepubescent boy raised by wolves who definitely did not have boobs? Yeah, I played him, no problem. At least it was a step up from playing a terrier.

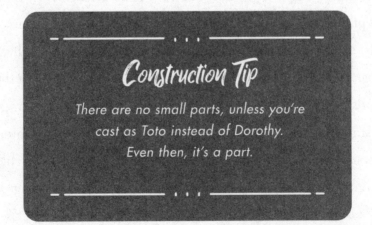

Construction Tip

There are no small parts, unless you're cast as Toto instead of Dorothy. Even then, it's a part.

During my senior year of high school, I was cast as Helen Keller in *The Miracle Worker*, a part I was ecstatic to play. I distinctly remember the drama teacher making a certain rehearsal mandatory, but I could not get off work that day. I pleaded with her to make an exception, but she gave me an ultimatum. I could not afford to lose my job, so I never got to play Helen. I was a year away from college and I was paying, so I didn't have much of a choice. I remember going to see that school play as a bitter party of one. The funny thing is, I was so upset at the time, but now I don't even remember who ended up playing that part. It's a good reminder that sometimes the things that seem horrible in the moment probably won't matter in the rearview. I had similar feelings years later when I watched an episode of *Law & Order* that had a guest role that I was supposed to play but couldn't, because I couldn't make it work with my *All My Children* schedule. I would rather be on an *All My Children* set than behind the counter at Dairy Queen, but the resentment was the same. I try to stay positive, but sometimes it's only human to feel a little pissed about a missed opportunity. I guess the lesson I learned early on is to honor your contracts and make responsible choices, like getting that paycheck that'll help you get through college, even if it's the less glamorous choice.

Those school plays, or even no-budget plays put on by the

local Baptist church, were the only times that I felt like I was good at something growing up. I got to be someone else, instead of being this person who was embarrassed or ashamed of my clothes or my house (or lack of house) or my looks. I loved the idea that I could play a character, and I realized I was good at it. I mean, barely any kids were going out for these plays, so the competition was slim. But I'd found something that I loved, and that became my way out. That, and reading books.

The way I grew up—moving constantly, house insecure, taking care of my younger siblings, and trying to help out financially—there wasn't a ton of space for me to be a child. Like I said, I had to buck up and become pretty resourceful and responsible at a young age. I guess there was a little Dakota Fanning in me, a kid who grew up faster than she should have in some ways. I will never forget my mom getting bleach on my favorite pair of jeans. It was not the cool kind of bleach that could possibly look like it was there on purpose, even though my mom tried to convince me of that. I asked her to teach me how to do laundry that very day, and I've done it myself ever since. I was ten.

When I was fifteen, my mom told me she was pregnant with her fifth child. We could barely afford the basic necessities like food and shelter, and she wanted to bring in *another* person to feed and clothe? It seemed so irresponsible to me, so I sat there lecturing *her* about unprotected sex and telling *her* we couldn't afford another kid. Who would pay for the doctor visits and diapers? I was already working and juggling so much, and I was honestly angry. I don't remember my mom getting upset with me, but I do know that I felt like a parent to her sometimes, and that was definitely one of those moments. Don't get me wrong, the second my baby sister entered this world I've never loved anyone more to this day, but at first, I was not on board with the idea.

This is when we lived in a one-bedroom duplex in Benton, Kentucky. Yes, the one that would later be the scene of a drive-by shooting. It had a cute entrance, complete with bullet holes that really helped with airflow since there was no AC and no heat. The shag carpet and linoleum really added to the charm. We had access to the eight-hundred-square-foot attic with exposed wood beams, and we slept up there when it wasn't too hot or too cold. I slept by the one window (natural light!), which had a gorgeous view of our broken-down car in the driveway. Otherwise my sisters and I piled in the living room to sleep. I always got the couch because of seniority. My younger sisters Tabatha and Charissa rotated between the chair and a pallet on the floor made of blankets. My oldest sister, Shonda, was off at college, so I was now the oldest sister, with the best attic view that money could buy at that time.

Shonda and I have always been close. She left our small town and married an amazing guy and now has incredible kids (maybe you've seen them on *Selling Sunset*). She owns her own spa, so she's a successful businesswoman, and she's kind of the anchor for our family now. If I can't remember something from our past, I call Shonda, and she's always there with the details. Tabatha and Charissa stayed in Kentucky. Tabatha is two years younger than I am, and she has three kids that she loves dearly. We fought a lot growing up and definitely had our ups and downs, but now we get along amazingly well. Charissa is two years younger than Tabatha and has two kids. She has the thickest southern accent of anyone in the family. She's a lot like our mom and loves the simple things in life, like sitting by a lake all day and enjoying the quiet. We could not have been more different as kids, but we've always gotten along. She was a total tomboy who loved lizards and snakes, and I was more interested in daytime soaps and auditioning for plays. Sabrina is the baby, and she has her aesthetician's license and has grown up to be one of the most beautiful, empathetic souls I've ever known. I'll probably always feel protective of her, since I literally took care of her since she was a newborn.

My parents did the best they could, like I said, but I definitely had to step in and act like a caretaker to my younger sisters. When my baby sister was born, I was often the one changing or feeding or burping her, which is probably why I wasn't rushing to have kids at a young age. I'd had the whole baby experience as a teenager, so as I got into my twenties I was more focused on my career. I studied in school, got As, never really got in trouble, and put a ton of energy into getting out and accomplishing these crazy dreams I had of becoming an actor—not just any actor, but an actor on a soap. The same soaps my mom and grandmother watched. My parents never discouraged my dreams, and I love them for that. When anyone doubted me along the way because of where I came from or who I was, I found a way to let the haters fuel me, to push me, and make me more determined to become one of those glamorous girls on a soap.

And now here we are.

I try not to make flash judgments about people, because so many people have done that to me, and it just strikes me as ridiculous. You *never* know what someone has experienced or even what kind of day they're having, so it doesn't serve either of you to assume you know where they're coming from. It was definitely funny when the girls at the slumber party at my grandmother's house assumed I was a "rich girl," just like it's funny to me when people see me now and assume I was born in a $20 million LA mansion, instead of being someone whose childhood was filled with eviction notices and who spent time living in an abandoned schoolhouse that had a leaky roof and a room full of old, creepy dolls in it.

We lived in that schoolhouse for a while when I was in high school, and to this day I cannot stand the smell of mildew. The collapsed roof meant that the old mattress I slept on was always a little wet and mildewy, and it was light-years away from the homes I now sell in LA. There were definitely no infinity pools or walk-in closets in that place. No utilities, but there was an old janitor's closet and some puddles of dirty water. In real estate we would call this a teardown and tout its great land value. We would sell it as an "investment opportunity." As a teenager, though, it was a source of deep humiliation for me. I was terrified people would find out we were actually squatting there. When I look back on things like this, it's even hard for ME to believe, and I was there. No matter where you come from or what your circumstances are, focus on what's important *to you*, and don't ever get down on yourself because you think someone else will judge you for overreaching.

Once you own who you are, the good and the bad, you can derive power from it, instead of shame. That acceptance is where real strength comes from. And maybe I blew off the role of Toto, but I did learn something from *The Wizard of Oz* after all. As Glinda the Good Witch said, "You've always had the power my dear . . . you just had to learn it for yourself."

CHAPTER TWO

So I Was a Walmart Barbie

Right now, my résumé would list notable things like Real Estate Agent, Actor, Host, Author, and *Dancing with the Stars* Contestant. But so many jobs came before those: Knife Salesperson, Promotional Walmart Barbie, Server, Hostess, Bartender, Hand Model, Rock Band Roadie, and Dairy Queen Manager. And that's only the beginning. Each job I've had over the years taught me a new skill, whether it was how to work a crowd (Walmart Barbie), how to hone a sales pitch (Knife Salesperson), or how to delegate (Dairy Queen Manager). I don't exactly miss all those early jobs, but I like to think they gave me *something* that I still use in my life and career today.

Take knife sales. If you think showing and selling multimillion-dollar homes in LA sounds like pressure, try walking up to people's front doors holding a bag of boning knives, cleavers, and kitchen shears—and asking total strangers to let you in! I was good at the job, even though once I was in a woman's kitchen trying to do our sales gimmick of cutting a penny in half with a knife, and the penny ended up flying across the room and breaking a vase. Luckily, she was sweet about it. Door-to-door knife sales was kind of a side hustle to make extra cash when I wasn't managing the local Dairy Queen in high school, and even though I'm pretty sure the knife job may have been some sort of pyramid scheme, I ended up being the top salesperson. Granted, it was a small office in Paducah, Kentucky, but still. The point is, I always knew how to hustle.

My first job, like that of many teens, was babysitting. Not exactly the kind you get paid for, but the kind where you were expected to do it and not complain. My first time getting an actual paycheck, as tiny as it was, was from working at the auto shop where my dad was a mechanic. I would ride to work with my dad, and they paid me $30 a week to answer phones from eight a.m. to five p.m. during the summer I was fifteen. Since my car knowledge was limited, I was constantly looking things up in a *Kelley Blue Book*, which is basically the biggest book you've ever seen, telling you the value of different cars and parts. People would call up and ask me how much a filter change would be for their 1992 Nissan Altima, and if I couldn't find it within a reasonable hold time I would just take my best guess at the cost. If the part sounded expensive, I'd say something like, "New brake pads will be about $200." I got in trouble pretty quickly, and my dad was not happy. I got a lecture about how I may have just driven precious customers to their rival shop, and so after that I was relegated to accepting deliveries and handing the adults the phone when it rang. Still, instead of partying all summer like the kids with social lives, I was clocking in and out of work and making money to save for college and help my family out. I also bought my first car with the work money I saved up: a $1,400 gray Pontiac Sunbird whose rusted paint job said it had been sitting in the sun for too long. I also had to use thumbtacks to keep the roof from caving in, but I didn't care. Nobody was prouder to have their own car than I was. I even hung air fresheners from Bath and Body Works to the rearview mirror to make it extra . . . special. I loved it. I didn't go anywhere besides school and work, really. Occasionally we would go to the mall, but malls aren't very fun when you have zero money to spend. Mostly, I just drove to work. I'm jealous of teenagers now who can start building an empire stuck in their rooms on TikTok. For me, there was no choice but to show up on time, do the job (even if I fabricated the prices of a few mufflers), and be responsible with my money.

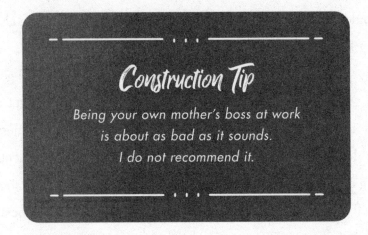

Construction Tip

*Being your own mother's boss at work
is about as bad as it sounds.
I do not recommend it.*

As you know by now, one of my more consistent jobs growing up was working at a Dairy Queen in Draffenville, Kentucky, a town so small it doesn't even have its own zip code. The DQ may as well have been a Michelin-star restaurant. Because I took the job seriously, showed up on time, and excelled at taking orders and filling milkshakes, I earned the respect of my boss. I was quickly promoted to manager. One of my duties was to take a bag full of cash to the bank after we closed each night, which, when I think about it, is actually really dangerous. The whole town was closed and here's this teenage girl all alone with a bunch of money. At the time, I didn't think anything of it. It was just work. Every night, the money was delivered to the bank, no problem. When they decided to open another DQ in Benton, a town just down the road, I was asked to help staff it. My mom needed a job, so I hired her, which ended up being a disaster. I'm pretty sure she could be crowned Worst DQ Employee of All Time. She filled the cones all wrong, putting mediums where the smalls were supposed to go, and larges in the small slots. This doesn't sound like a big deal until you imagine going to pull what is supposed to be a small cone out of the designated small hole, and because the large cones are too big to fit through, your cone explodes everywhere when pulled. The thing was, when I showed her *again* how to fill product, she just didn't give a damn! "Give me a break, Terrina, who really cares," she'd say. Looking back now I can laugh, but at the time I had other employees coming up to me and secretly saying, "Terrina, *your mom*."

Her lack of adherence to the rules annoyed me, but I admire her defiance now. No one could own that woman. She was always the boss. Like I said before, one day while plugging away at the local DQ I caught her smoking a cigarette while working the drive-through window. She'd steal condiments, disappear from her shift, and then just wander back when she felt like it, and I was the manager so I was the one who had to reprimand her! In the end I had to fire my own mother from Dairy Queen, because it wasn't really fair to the other employees if I gave my mom a pass for missing shifts or smoking at the drive-through window. I think me telling her that it wasn't working out happened about one minute before she was about to quit anyway. We laughed about this for years, but she'd still never admit that she was wrong for the way she filled the cones. I didn't realize it as a teenager, but as I got older I saw my mom as a fucking legend. I stopped being ashamed and was able to find so much humor in her attitude. I didn't adopt that defiance at work—I wasn't stealing props from the *All My Children* set or walking away from work for a smoke break—but I do think it's important to know when to stand up for yourself and act like a boss even when you're not one. Responsibly, of course.

I saved for college and ended up going to Murray State University in Kentucky. I waited tables, and I helped build sets for plays for about five bucks an hour to pay my tuition and living expenses. I heard about an on-campus job making ten bucks an hour being a nude model for art classes, so I decided why not double my income? I asked a drama teacher I trusted whether or not I should do it, and she basically said the human body is a beautiful thing. So I told myself, *This is art!* There was nothing sexual about it at all. You stand there, freezing, trying to stay still and not sneeze or scratch your arm. The art students were all respectful and more interested in drawing my hand correctly than ogling me, but the safe feeling in the room didn't last long. One day I glanced at the door and realized that kids outside the class by the elevator could see inside, and that they *were* staring and laughing. I completely froze, even more than I already was. I don't know why I didn't say anything right then, but I quit right after that. The teacher tried to get me to come back—unsurprisingly I guess there's a shortage of people who want to stand around in their birthday suit in a classroom—but I was done.

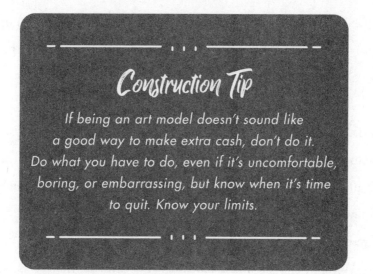

Construction Tip

If being an art model doesn't sound like a good way to make extra cash, don't do it. Do what you have to do, even if it's uncomfortable, boring, or embarrassing, but know when it's time to quit. Know your limits.

I have waited on so many tables in my life, and I'm pretty sure I was a server at every single restaurant within twenty miles of my college. I carried trays full of beer to rowdy college students at a place called Fifteenth & Olive, and I served porterhouses and martinis at a high-class steak house, The Bull Pen. It was the fanciest restaurant within a one-hour radius. That's when

I learned *not* to tell people that I was a theater major. People would ask what my major was, and I got sick of their condescending comments every time I told the truth about my plan to move to LA to be an actor. "Out of everyone that moves there and fails, what makes you think you'll be any different?" "What's your backup plan if and when it doesn't work out?" Magically, as soon as I started telling them I was a business major, the questions and condescending comments stopped. I got an approving nod and we moved right on to how they wanted their steak cooked. I found it much easier to stay focused and do my job if I protected myself and kept my acting aspirations a secret. I didn't know whether I was going to go off and be a successful actor, but I knew I was going to try. There was nothing they could have said to stop me, but I didn't need the comments. Maybe I got that from my mom: Who cares what they think? I'm doing what I want! Right after I serve this rib eye.

While the steak house job wasn't my favorite, there was one job I had in college that, looking back, was kind of a foreshadowing of my future. Since I was trying to up my income, I was always on the lookout for new opportunities. One day I spotted a post on a bulletin board advertising $100 a day to dress as a Barbie at local Walmarts. You're basically a "promo girl," like the women who walk around at bars handing out Red Bull or Budweiser. I had several of those jobs over the years. I called about the Barbie job, and they hired me even though I didn't exactly look the part. I had dark brown hair, and Barbies back then mostly had blond hair and blue eyes. They sent me a one-size-fits-all pink costume made out of fake satin, complete with an elastic waistband. It looked like a wrinkled Halloween costume. Since so many little girls love Barbie, I thought it would be fun to have my little sister Sabrina come visit me in the Walmart Barbie costume. But she was a tomboy at the time and wanted nothing to do with Barbie, so unlike all the other little girls who worshipped me as Barbie, my own sister was not impressed at all. The costume didn't quite have the impact I was going for.

The job entailed showing up at Walmart to help boost their sales by signing Barbie doll boxes, always making sure to dot the *I* in Barbie with a heart (hey, it was a job requirement). Despite what it might sound like, I actually thought this job was cool. I would sit at a table, just like I did several years later for soap events, and sign autographs, only back then I was signing *Barbie*. Years later when I was on *All My Children* and someone actually did ask me for my autograph, I remember being so confused. Even though I'd signed "autographs" as Barbie, I never imagined that someone would want me to sign *Chrishell*. It was so bizarre at first, I actually asked the person, "You mean, just write my name?" Signing my own name was a whole different experience than writing *Barbie*. I had so much fun getting into character and making little kids happy, I even considered traveling to Walmarts in other states. Once I found out I'd have to pay for my own gas, though, the roaming Barbie idea was out. I had bills to pay.

Despite what all those patrons at the steak house said, once I graduated from college I packed up my red Chevy Cavalier and drove straight to Los Angeles to chase my dream. My college boyfriend and I found a temporary room for one month via Craigslist, and we had the sunroom in a house where a guy who was very proud of his career in porn (and told us to check it out) rented the couch. We had great natural light, and zero privacy. When I got there, I juggled multiple jobs at once. Then I moved into a small shared apartment with one of my Tony Roma's coworkers that was worlds away from the glam homes you see on *Selling Sunset*. We had a three-bedroom, two-bath place in Burbank, and I had a tiny balcony off my bedroom that was just big enough to stand on. It didn't even fit a chair. The place had zero personality, but what did I care at the time? I was living in Los Angeles.

It wasn't that tough to get a job waiting tables in Murray, Kentucky, so I was a little shocked when I got to LA and discovered that there was a hierarchy at restaurants unless you knew someone. (I didn't.) This is the land of Sur and TomTom, and landing a server or bartending job at one of these places is like winning the lottery. Those came along after my waitressing days, but I quickly learned you have to pay your dues as a hostess in Los Angeles, and when a server job opens up, you might get it if you're lucky. I was never one to sit around and wait, though.

I got a hostess job at Tony Roma's at Universal CityWalk, which was teeming with a mix of tourists and locals, especially after concerts let out. Servers make more than hostesses, so I had my eye on a server job even though I was last in line as the new girl. I noticed other servers struggling to keep up when we were slammed, so I begged the manager to give me a few tables. Maybe my time in knife sales came in handy, because my pitch eventually worked when a server didn't show up right as a Blue Man Group concert was letting out. I asked the manager to give me two tables, and I said if I messed up I would never bug him about it again. I put my server skills to use, and I also told the people I waited on that instead of tipping me, I'd love for them to go up to the manager as they were leaving and tell him how much they loved me. It did piss off the other hostesses a little bit, but this was about survival—and paying rent. They were mostly young high school kids living with their parents, whereas I was a few hundred dollars away from living on the street. So after that night I didn't hostess anymore, I remained friends with the other hostesses, and my rent was paid. Just like way back when I asked the newscaster

Amy Watson if I could shadow her, I took the initiative and made something happen. I refused to sit at that hostess stand night after night, waiting for my turn to make a living. I saw an in, and I took it.

Before I landed my role on *All My Children,* I was working three jobs that were spread all over the city, from the Westside to the Valley. If you've ever lived in Los Angeles or experienced its freeways, you know this is a terrible idea. I was so excited to be in California, going after my lifelong dream, that the traffic didn't bother me. I worked as a camp counselor at a beach in Pacific Palisades basically babysitting the kids of celebrities and blockbuster directors. It was a flexible job, which allowed me to go to auditions when I needed to. Then there was Tony Roma's, and I'd change clothes in the car on my long drive out to Universal Studios. After Tony Roma's, for a while I worked the night shift as a hand model on an Ultimate Shopping Network (USN) show selling jewelry. That job went from nine p.m. to six a.m., and I'd drive home to Burbank in the morning and try to sleep before it was time to get back in the car and head to the camp in the Palisades again. My sleep schedule was a disaster, but my manicures, paid for by the third job, were on point.

The hand model job came about after I answered an ad on some actor website. I got a manicure and went to the interview, and apparently I had what it took to become a hand model. There

I was, late at night, modeling bracelets and rings and rotating a wheel of necklaces. I also told the host that I knew everything there was to know about jewelry, even though I knew nothing. I even said my parents owned a jewelry store! I knew my destiny was to actually have my *face* on camera, so just like at Tony Roma's, I begged the host, let's call him Ron, to give me a chance on camera. Ron would always leave in the middle of the show for cigarette breaks, and since it was live, the camera would just play music and show the jewelry in his absence. It must have been so boring for the people at home. Ron kept brushing me off, but I guess I convinced him or annoyed him enough that when I asked him to give me one shot on camera to prove myself, he eventually relented. I told him that if I sold one piece of jewelry, great, and if not, I would never ask him again. This tactic was becoming a pattern, and it worked.

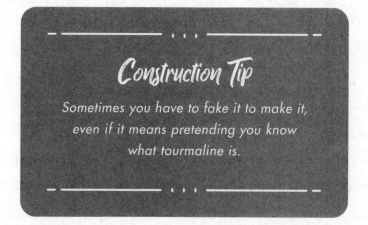

Construction Tip

Sometimes you have to fake it to make it, even if it means pretending you know what tourmaline is.

When Ron left for his next smoke break, I pulled out all the stops. I waxed poetic in my thick Kentucky accent about the tourmaline and rose quartz, and the showcase piece: a pearl bracelet on an elastic band. Seeing my in, I spoke straight to the audience and said, "Guys, you have to help me out." On live TV, I told the audience that this was my one shot to sell some jewelry, and guess what? It worked. I sold more than one piece, Ron was impressed, and from that night on I got to cohost the show. To prepare for the part, I googled terms I heard Ron say and printed out a list so I could throw around buzzwords like *gallery, clarity,* and *tanzanite*. I learned all the tricks they used to make blue stones look bluer or to add more sparkle, and based on what I now know, please don't ever buy jewelry off a rotating wheel on a late night cable show. Ron and I would banter back and forth, and even though I was a costar, I still got paid my tiny hand model rate. Looking back, I should have asked for a raise, but that was a lesson I had yet to learn: know your value, and ask for it.

In between hustling to pay rent, I went on auditions. One gave me the opportunity to meet an amazing casting director named Judy Blye Wilson who was southern and so sweet, and she's a friend to this day. She discovered people like Josh Duhamel and Sarah Michelle Gellar and Cameron Mathison, and she had such a different energy than other casting directors. You really felt like she was rooting for you, which in most LA audition rooms, isn't the norm. She saw something in me back then and was so instrumental in helping to start my career. On my audition with Judy, I was auditioning to play Sydney Fox on *All My Children*, which I would later learn was Amanda Dillon. Amanda was a beloved character and had been on the show as a little girl, and she was now going to be returning as a scheming adult. At the time I didn't know that it was common for them to use pseudonyms or fake you out about which role you're actually auditioning for, and it was a secret that Amanda was going to come back on the show after so many years, so they were trying to keep it confidential. I got callbacks in LA, which means they like you enough to ask you back to audition again. This was my first soap audition, and the first big role I had ever gone out for. Then I got a call that I was being *flown to New York* to screen-test, which is basically to audition on camera. When I got to New York, there was a welcome packet with *Confidential* printed on it, and inside were the script pages showing that I was actually auditioning to play Amanda. I remember one particular strawberry blond actress at the audition who was so mean, and she kept trying to get in our heads and psych us out so we'd screw up our screen tests. Even though I wanted anyone but her to get the job, I assumed she would since she seemed so confident. With more experience I've learned that the loudest person in the room isn't always the most confident, or competent.

I could not believe I had been flown to New York City to screen-test for a four-year contract role on *All My Children*. I'd auditioned for so many "girl washing her face" or "girl driving car" commercial roles, it was hard to believe that THIS could be the first thing I booked. It seemed impossible. So impossible that I figured if nothing else, I was getting a free, fun trip to a city I'd always wanted to see, and at least I knew I was on the right path. For that reason, I wasn't as nervous as I would have been if I had convinced myself I *had* to get this job. I was just thrilled to have a per diem and to eat my first slice of real New York pizza and to stay at the Hotel Beacon on the Upper West Side. It was by far the coolest thing that had ever happened to me. Whether I got the role or not, the experience was a dream come true.

Going into this job thinking I'd already won, in a sense, helped me stay calm under pressure. I didn't walk into that screen test full of nerves, feeling like if I didn't get the part, it was all over. It's easier said than done, but for any job or audition, try to walk in there like you've already won something. Because I felt so calm and I wasn't visibly trembling, causing script pages to shake in my hands like so many times before, I just did the job I went there to do. At one point, the director,

Steven Williford, leaned over to me and said, "You're nailing this." I was like, "Wait, really?" That was a major confidence boost and exactly what I needed to truly own the moment. I left New York not knowing whether or not I got the job, but I felt like I'd given it everything I had, and I'd done it in an authentic way. But then, the wait . . .

I had auditioned the Thursday before Labor Day, and the casting director told me that since it was a holiday weekend I wouldn't hear anything until Tuesday at the earliest. That's an excruciatingly long time to sit around and wait for a call, so I tried my best to distract myself. Monday came along, and the phone rang. It was my manager.

"Pack your bags," she said.

"That's not funny!" It wasn't Tuesday, so this couldn't be real, I thought. My manager said she was serious, and I literally started screaming. I was jumping on my bed, crying and in total shock. Even writing about it now, I still get chills. It was a once-in-a-lifetime moment. I had just proven to every single person who ever doubted me that I could do it, and shown the people who had believed in me that they were right. No matter what else has happened or will happen in my life, that is THE most defining moment. I can still play it back in my head and feel that joy all over again.

That night I headed back to Tony Roma's to turn in my

apron. After saying my goodbyes, I went out to celebrate with my coworkers at a dueling piano bar next door, where we'd always get a discount. The bar was called Howl at the Moon, and I remember feeling nervous and excited and more than ready for the next phase of my life, and whatever it was that lay ahead. When I took the server apron off that night, I was hoping it would be the last time I would ever wear that uniform, because I was ready for a costume change.

Best (and Worst) Jobs Ever

You can learn something from any job you have, whether you're a server, a soap star, a Walmart Barbie, or a Realtor. Here are some of my best and worst jobs, and the lessons I took from each one.

Auto Mechanic Receptionist: Fake it till you make it. You may not always feel like you are great at your job, but sometimes acting like you belong there is half the battle.

Roadie: My knowledge of classic rock is pretty impressive, and it tends to come in handy on the occasional drunken karaoke night.

Selling Knives Door-to-Door: I am still in sales now, just on a much bigger scale. In my toughest moments I like to remember: if I could be invited into a stranger's home with a bag full of knives and close a sale, I can sell anything.

Dairy Queen Manager: With great power comes great responsibility, like having to fire your own mom when you're her boss. I also still love anywhere with self-serve ice cream, so I can take pride in the fact that I perfected my curlicue on top.

Theater Set Construction: Measure twice, cut once. Also I learned how to reupholster, which would come in handy when trying to make something old look great on a budget.

Walmart Barbie: If you have the ability to make someone's day, do it. People come up often asking for pictures and not always at the best time. Remember how hard you worked to get here, and be grateful for people going out of their way to say something nice, always.

Server: Don't wait for things to fall in your lap. If you want a promotion, find a way to get it, like convincing the manager to give you two tables even though you're "just" a hostess.

Hand Model: There are no small jobs. Take pride in your work (and manicure if that's applicable). It could always lead to your next big step.

Soap Star: Hardest job in television. Strong work ethic is a must, and being able to memorize lines and work off the cuff has come in handy more times than I could count.

Professional Dancer (Sort Of): Sometimes the things that scare you the most are what you should be doing. Get out of your box and say yes to new things. It could be just what you need.

Realtor: Working for yourself requires tremendous discipline but can be the most rewarding experience. Bet on yourself always.

CHAPTER THREE

The Power of the Flip

*W*hen we filmed my part for the opening sequence of *All My Children*, I was told to flip my hair. You know, that dramatic over-the-shoulder turn you see women do in daytime soap operas or on the cover of romance novels. When the director asked me to do "the flip" for the first time, it felt like an out-of-body experience. I'd been rehearsing my flip since I was a wayward-toothed little girl in Kentucky, imitating the stars I watched on soaps. All those days spent tossing my hair in the mirror paid off. It seemed like I willed it—or flipped it—into becoming a reality.

Obviously it takes more than mugging in a mirror, or merely wishing your dreams are going to come true, to make them come true. I was also obsessed with nailing Whitney Houston's rendition of "I Will Always Love You," and yeah, that was never going to happen. But one of the great things about being a kid is that you don't see limits, you just try. When you're a kid, the world hasn't corrupted you with fears and expectations yet, and the goal is to try to hold on to that childlike confidence as you get older. When you ask a kid what they want to be when they grow up, they aren't thinking about logistics. There is such an innocent beauty to their answers, and my answer to "What do you want to be?" was to be on a soap opera. If I hadn't watched *Guiding Light* and *The Young and the Restless* with my mom and grandmother, I still think I would have pursued acting, but I might not have been so genre specific. And luckily for me, that panned out much better than my wish to wake up with Whitney Houston's vocal cords.

My mom didn't mind my flair for the theater because I kept all her kids busy by forcing my sisters to act in plays I directed. My sisters hated every minute, but our musical theater rendition of Tim McGraw's "Don't Take the Girl" was award-worthy in my thirteen-year-old mind. Of course, I always cast myself in the lead role, and my sisters were there to begrudgingly act as my supporting cast. I also remember sitting around the house (when we had a house) and reading newspaper advertisements front to back as if I were on a TV commercial. "This week at Piggly Wiggly, bone-in ham only $5.99!" or "Hurry in and buy one sheet cake, get one free!" Hard to imagine a more annoying kid. I remember once reading an ad insert out loud all the way through to the end and flipping it back over to start again, and when I did, my mom finally lost it. "That's it! Go outside and play!" At some point I realized most people on TV sounded very different from me with my southern drawl. I practiced emulating newscasters to try to get rid of my southern accent, mimicking their regionless, flat dialect. I would practice and repeat what they said, because I definitely didn't have money for a dialect coach. I wouldn't even learn that a dialect coach was a thing until college.

As proof of how serious I was, I have a photo from my senior year of high school that shows me beaming and holding a large check for $1,000. I'd seen a flyer posted at a café advertising an acting contest for men only where you had to send in a tape of yourself doing a scene from a play or film, and the winner got $1,000 in college scholarship money. I made sure to read the fine print (pro tip: ALWAYS read the fine print before entering contests), and what do you know, it said women *could* enter. So I recruited a guy from my theater class to play Rhett Butler to my Scarlett O'Hara in a scene from *Gone with the Wind*, we filmed it, and I sent it in. I figured you could not get much more dramatic than Scarlett, and it was an iconic scene from the movie. The people running the contest asked me if my scene partner would like to enter as well, but he was two years younger than me and dressed like his family would be paying for his college, which might sound bad, but that's how I was framing it in my head. I was threatened by the question because they used an actual picture of Rhett Butler to announce the contest, and I assumed they probably wanted a guy to win a male acting contest after all. I couldn't afford to lessen my chances of winning, so I rationalized telling them he didn't want to be entered by telling myself that I was the one who found and researched the contest, sourced the costumes, and put the whole video together. He really was doing it as a favor to me. But I still should have asked him. The stress of needing to pay for college sometimes meant needing to be scrappy, and to look out for myself, and that's exactly what I did. My competitive side had come out, but it paid off, literally. I put that money toward tuition and classes, and I also got something just as important from that win: a much-needed boost of confidence to continue down the path toward my dream.

Construction Tip

*Always—and I mean always—
read the fine print.*

In college, I started to transition out of my "ugly duckling" phase. I realized that if I wanted to have the best shot at making it as an actor, I needed to fix my teeth, lose my accent, and grow out my hair. But it had to get worse before it got better. Four words: Clear. Braces. Freshman. Year. Dr. Woods let me do a payment plan of $200 a month, and I could only afford to fix my top teeth. If you look closely, I still have a crooked tooth on the bottom, but I figured since you didn't really see it, it wasn't worth another $2,000 that I didn't have. My chances of finding and winning two more acting contests that paid $1,000 each didn't seem super high.

When I graduated from Murray State University and told my parents I would be moving to LA, I found it amusing that they were surprised. It was sweet and endearing to find out my mom thought I was going to move back with them in their tiny trailer. Because the truth was, the second I left for college I knew I would never be back. Back to visit, sure, but the next time I called a trailer mine would be on a Hollywood lot somewhere.

I always teetered about whether a four-year degree was the right move for an actor, so by the time I graduated I was aching to head west. I already felt behind as far as auditions and networking, and there was no time to waste. So I packed up my Cavalier and off I went with my college boyfriend, who was an incredibly sweet guy who was into music and who treated me like gold. We loved each other, so we decided to see how life in LA would work out for us, even though he was a Kentucky kid at heart. On the drive west, we stayed at the shittiest motels imaginable. Places that catered to truckers, one-hour hotel renters, and spiders. If I saw a place that cost $49.99 a night and another place across the street that was $39.99, we would always go with the cheaper option. I'm not sure if that $10 would have made a difference or not, but I reminded myself I had slept in worse conditions and just tried to touch as little as possible. That's why it helps to pursue your dreams while you're young and before you've developed a healthy fear of bedbugs, serial killers, and brown shower water, and you have enough sense not to choose the $39.99 room to save ten bucks, if you can help it.

I remember driving into Los Angeles and instantly falling in love with the city. I had never seen a real palm tree in person before, let alone hundreds of them. I made us stop so I could take a photo on the side of the road, standing next to one. I was a total tourist, and so incredibly excited to be there. I ended up renting a small, crappy apartment in the worst, seediest section of North Hollywood, but because my new address had "Hollywood" in it, it was as glamorous to me as the land of 90210.

Sitting on Mom's lap, holding a Busch beer with a pull tab. It was a different time. 😆 😆 😆

Photo courtesy of Jeff Stause

In our household it didn't matter if you weren't tall enough to reach the sink, the dishes still had to be done. Here I am on a step stool happily finishing my chores.

Photo courtesy of Jeff Stause

Secondhand smoke and Mountain Dew in a Chaffee Red Devils cup from the town where I was born. Pretty normal in those days. #childhood 😆

Photo courtesy of Jeff Stause

Me (in the middle) with my sisters Tabatha and Charissa.
Photo courtesy of Ranae Stause

Posing in a photo booth with my older sister, Shonda. This is from the phase where one of my front teeth started to go rogue and I became too self-conscious to smile. 😝

Throwback photos are always fun for those moments when you think, *What the hell was I thinking with that haircut and perm?*
Photo courtesy of Erma Stause

Beaming because I won a male-only acting contest my senior year of high school and got some money to pay for college.
Photo courtesy of Ranae Stause

Mom with Shonda, me, and Sabrina.
Photo courtesy of Erma Stause

My sisters Charissa (in white) and Tabatha (in pink) had a
double wedding. Tabatha originally wanted to do a camouflage-themed
wedding, and to this day it's one of my biggest regrets that
I talked her out of it. The photos would've been epic!
Photo courtesy of Erma Stause

With my lifelong crush Jordan Knight when New Kids on the Block performed on *The View*. I went into work at *All My Children* to get my hair and makeup done for this very moment!
Photo courtesy of Christina Gan

All My Children Halloween party in New York. I was Catwoman, but this is a few drinks later, so clearly I lost the mask.
Photo courtesy of Christina Gan

My set construction days at college (before I learned how to sit up straight).
Photo courtesy of David Balthrop

Posing with other cast members when I played Cecily in
The Importance of Being Ernest during college.
Photo courtesy of David Balthrop

Back in Kentucky with my best friends from college, Julie and Elly.
Photo courtesy of Shevonne Sullivan

Back home in Kentucky
visiting my mom.
Photo courtesy of Shonda Davisson

With my parents, sister, and aunt and uncle having dinner at the local Ponderosa in Kentucky where my little sister Sabrina worked. I didn't know it at the time, but this would be the last photo I took with my dad.

Photo courtesy of Shonda Davisson

Mom and Dad at their favorite restaurant, Patti's, in Kentucky.

Photo courtesy of Chrishell Stause

Shonda, Sabrina, and me wearing our rock T-shirts at
my dad's memorial. We were heartbroken, but we tried
to turn the day into a celebration of his life.
Photo courtesy of Chris Davisson

Me and Sabrina keeping our mom's spirits up while she was getting chemo.

Photo courtesy of Shonda Davisson

With Mom at the cabin in Kentucky that we took her to during chemo. I brought this wig from LA and she just loved it. 💚

Photo courtesy of Sabrina Stause

At *Dancing with the Stars*, the hair and makeup team was always on point, even if my dancing wasn't.
Photo courtesy of Chrishell Stause

In the rehearsal room the first week of *Dancing with the Stars*, right before I was about to try to tackle a tango.
Photo courtesy of Chrishell Stause

In full makeup to dance as Maleficent on *Dancing with the Stars*. They told me not to smile or it would mess up the prosthetic. So here's me trying to channel my best Angelina that day.
Photo courtesy of Chrishell Stause

With Sabrina and Shonda during Christmas 2020.
Photo courtesy of Chris Davisson

Selling Sunset season four team meeting at the office. You can spot some of the production equipment in the background.

Photo courtesy of Sean Bjordal

During *Selling Sunset* season four, we went dress shopping for a joint birthday party, and Mary and I ended up loving the same dress. We were going to throw a themed birthday party until we realized production wasn't going to foot the bill. So we just took a pic for the Gram.

Photo courtesy of Sean Bjordal

At the gym with Amanza. She hated to workout so we took a bunch of photos instead.

Photo courtesy of Chrishell Stause

With Brett, Jason, Mary, and the new agents, Emma and Vanessa, during season four of *Selling Sunset* at one of my listings in the Valley.
Photo courtesy of Sean Bjordal

Niko and Zelda's birthday party at one of Jason's listings. We had everyone bring donations for the local dog shelter.
Photo courtesy of Sean Bjordal

Headed to Capri for the day in a helicopter. I was so nervous. I was trying to look like I wasn't about to pee my pants in this photo.

Photo courtesy of Romain Bonnet

On our balcony in Positano. We took this photo the day before we shared our status with the world. Fun fact: this is Jason's phone wallpaper.

Photo courtesy of Chrishell Stause

That boyfriend decided California wasn't for him and he headed home to Kentucky, so by the time we hit Los Angeles our relationship lasted about as long as an Erica Kane marriage (for those who aren't soap buffs, think Kim Kardashian and Kris Humphries). I was sad but not crushed by the breakup, even though he was an amazing guy. I had dreams to fulfill, tables to wait, auditions to go on, and eventually, a soap opera to book. I ended up finding a manager who turned out to be pretty shady and predatory, which is a common story among many new actors in Los Angeles. These managers promise you'll become a star and that they have all the connections, but really they're out to take your money and waste your time. Eventually I figured out that my manager was horrible at contracts and negotiations and that I was getting a raw deal, but it took a while to wise up to that.

I spent about a year waiting tables in LA, and once I was cast on *All My Children*, I sold the Chevy on Craigslist and moved to New York, another city that was wildly glamorous, and a little scary, to me. I remember telling my mom about the job, and she was excited, but as a die-hard *Y&R* fan, she managed to add, "That's great that you're on TV, baby doll, but can you get on *The Young and the Restless*?" Eventually I did, but still. My mom was very loyal to her show, as so many devoted soap fans are. For some, loving a certain soap is like rooting for your favorite sports team, and when a character is killed off, it's like LeBron being traded. So without my mom even knowing, she planted a seed in my head that getting on *Y&R* would become a major goal of mine. I guess you never stop trying to impress your parents.

After all the manifesting and hair flipping, combined with dogged determination, there I was in New York, on the set of *All My Children* for the first day of shooting. The casting director taped it, which is customary, so I have a behind-the-scenes video on VHS. Imagine walking in for your first day, heading to wardrobe, and finding out that your first ever on-camera ensemble as a professional actor is . . . lingerie. I was supposed to jump out of bed in the scene, and then stand there and act in front of the cameras wearing next to nothing. I was so nervous, but knew I just had to dive in headfirst. It was an out-of-body experience. There I was, looking down at my body, very out there. I didn't know it at the time, but I guess I'd been preparing for the scene during those few days as a nude art model in college. I didn't have a DVR in my hotel room and my episodes always aired during the day while I was working, so I didn't see myself on camera much, thank goodness. I was so green and I had no idea how to work with the cameras or the lighting, so seeing myself might have killed my confidence. I'm also thankful that social media wasn't the monster that it is now back in 2005, because lord knows the trolls would have come out from under their bridges. I was playing a character that fans had loved long before, when she was a sweet little blond girl, and here I was, this new person, playing the character as a grown-up, manipulative party girl. There were blog posts and message boards about how much some people hated me, and I remember walking in New York one day and a woman on the street started SCREAMING at me, saying that Amanda (my character) was so awful to Lily. She definitely thought that I was *actually* Amanda, so I guess that's a compliment?

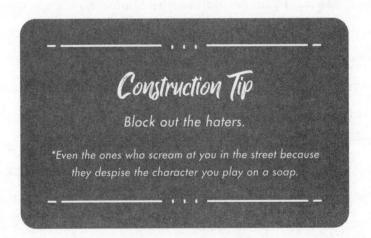

Construction Tip

Block out the haters.

*Even the ones who scream at you in the street because they despise the character you play on a soap.

At first, getting emotional on camera was really hard for me. There was a scene where Amanda was supposed to be tricking the character J.R. by bursting into tears to gain sympathy from him. I couldn't do it, and it felt like people on set were taking notice. I felt like they were thinking, *Maybe this new girl will just be part of the young, scantily clad crowd we bring in for the summer.* It felt as if they were watching to see if I would sink or swim. Luckily my character was *supposed* to be fake crying, so it worked out. A little later, when they brought in an actress named Kate Collins to play my character's crazy mom, I was pleasantly surprised that she treated me like a real daughter off camera, and I was (and still am) a moth to a flame with any sort of mothering, nurturing energy. My own mom struggled with bipolar disorder and depression her whole life, and here was my TV mom dealing with similar issues, obviously in a more dramatic, daytime TV way. Kate and I connected off camera, and it was the first time my real life informed my scenes, so all of a sudden our story line soared. I have been crying on cue in scripted TV ever since. I love scripted scenes where I can really play the emotion of a character. The only time I'm uncomfortable now is when I have to play myself. I wish I could tell you the tears on *Selling Sunset* are performative, but unfortunately those are the effects of real life, happening in real time. I'd much rather cry on a soap.

Eventually, I found my sea legs, and the blog posts or angry fans didn't bother me as much. I was working at my absolute dream job. I'll never forget my first time being at

the Daytime Emmys and running into the actress Lauralee
Bell, who played Cricket (she now goes by Christine) on *The
Young and the Restless*. I idolized her as a kid, and I would
watch her scenes or opening montages thinking she and the
other soap stars were the most glamorous women I'd ever
seen. I went from worshipping these people as faraway idols
to actually working with some of them. Besides the hair flip,
I remember some of the women having their hair in slick
ponytails with a strand of hair wrapped around to disguise
the hair band. It seems so simple now but back then it was
groundbreaking to me, and I tried (and failed) to do that
with my own hair. I was just transfixed by these women and
their hairstyles, like some girls are with Barbies. When I did
end up working with some of them, I was usually too embarrassed to gush and tell them how much I loved them as a kid.
Plus, that's not something you really want to say to a woman
who's older than you: *Hey, I grew up watching you. Big fan,
HUGE!* Instead, I just kept my fandom to myself and tried
to look professional, even though I was bursting with nerves
and excitement inside. I got to work with the biggest names
in daytime, people like Susan Lucci, Debbi Morgan, Deidre
Hall, Eric Braeden, Kristian Alfonso, and Michael Knight, to
name a few. But I still felt like that little kid, idolizing them
and their beautiful hair.

Construction Tip

If you're feeling nervous at work, remember that people at the top were once in your position. Everyone starts somewhere.

Over the years I got to know icons like Susan Lucci, whom I love on a personal level. She's a consummate professional and so funny. I was twenty-three years old when I started the show, so of course I was extremely nervous to say hello to her, or even make eye contact at first. I asked another actor to introduce me to her, and when we got to know each other a little bit she asked if I was single. She said she had a friend she wanted to introduce me to, and she invited me to dinner with them. I didn't care about the guy—I was having dinner with Susan Lucci, aka Erica freaking Kane!

Susan was launching a new clothing line, and she'd asked me to model some of the clothes on *The View*. Her friend had seen me on the show and asked Susan to introduce us. I hadn't been in New York for long, and I had never in my life eaten at a fancy restaurant. In the cab on the way to the restaurant,

I frantically called my older sister to see if she could help me decipher the French menu, since I didn't speak French and this was the first time I was seeing phrases like *foie gras* or *le fromage*. The only one I understood was *le dessert*. However, that night I learned the hard way that sweetbreads are not actually sweet or bread.

"What do I order?! Just tell me where the chicken is," I asked her frantically. I did not want to sound like an uncultured Kentucky hick in front of Susan Lucci/Erica Kane.

"Just get the cordon bleu," she said. "That's the chicken."

So I walk into the fancy French restaurant, and there's Susan, and there's her friend, who is much older than me. And I'm being generous. It was still exciting to be at a nice restaurant with one of my childhood idols, and I remember Susan asking me if I liked truffles and sweetbreads, and me responding, "Sure!" I had no clue what I was eating, and I'm just glad I didn't know "delicacies" like sweetbreads are basically the glands of calves and lambs. I haven't eaten them since the day I found out, which was the day after that dinner when I called Shonda to ask her what I'd eaten. As soon as she told me, I wanted to vomit.

Later, when Susan realized how young I was, she apologized for the setup and felt awful. She said she assumed I was older because I seemed so mature for my age. She was so embarrassed, but we still laugh about it today. It wasn't her best matchmaking attempt, but at least I got a good dinner out of it (minus the sweetbreads).

I met so many longtime friends working on soaps, from actors and directors to producers and crew. I even met my ex-husband when I was working on *Days of Our Lives*, which is a story for another time (and another chapter). I became an actor, I flipped my hair, and I earned my first real acting money (more on that later too). I still sometimes pinch myself that this happened, even though I worked so hard and believed so strongly that it would.

My mom came out to see me in New York when I was still newish to *All My Children*, and she got to sit on set and watch us film. It sounds exciting, and for an hour or so it actually is, but if you've ever been on a TV or movie set, you know that the hours can drag on. It was a normal occurrence for me to be on set over twelve hours a day. She managed to stay the whole time that first day, but after that she was done. The following day I had a New York tourist itinerary all written out for her, so she could walk around and see the Empire State Building or the Statue of Liberty or Times Square, but Mom was not having it. She hated the city, so instead of exploring we ended up buying plants and flowers and turning the little balcony off my apartment into an outdoor oasis. It was so sweet of her, but I also couldn't understand how she could stay inside all day in New York City! I loved the city so much that my heart beat faster when I looked up at the tall buildings or the bustle on the streets. You could not have kept me inside by chaining me down if I had a day in New York to myself. I would have busted out and gone sightseeing for sure.

I loved walking around New York City, exploring the streets, and trying different restaurants, especially since my exposure to restaurants before this mostly included buffets and me waiting tables. I would sometimes walk from my apartment on Fourth Street to work on Sixty-Sixth Street. No one walks in LA, and if you've seen our footwear on *Selling Sunset* you can probably see why. I loved it in New York, though. I also did every touristy thing you could do, and I tried to get my mom to go out and do the same. She was such a nature-loving flower child, though, so seeing Times Square was not her thing. I do wish I had "before" and "after" photos of my little balcony in New York. She really made it look magical. That apartment was the most I had ever spent on a place to live. I think it was about $3,000 a month, in Manhattan, and it had that cute balcony, which is major in New York. My idea of what is "major" in real estate is a little different now, but that apartment made me feel like I had truly made it at the time.

Working on *All My Children* was like graduate school for me. I grew as a person and an actor, my costars and producers and directors became like family, and it was such an intense bonding time, and then one day it was suddenly just . . . over.

For almost seven years, I had my dream job. Then the show moved to LA in 2010 and was eventually canceled. When it ended, I think, because it was my first job, I assumed all jobs would be so tight-knit and fulfilling. That show means so much to me because it's where I found my self-confidence and made so many amazing friendships. I always think of those days fondly, even if my wardrobe sometimes left a lot to be desired and not much to the imagination. I guess that's what your twenties are for. I remember the first day I sat in the hair and makeup chair on the show. When I looked in the mirror at the finished product, I gasped. "I can look like this?!" I'd never had my hair and makeup done, and if you saw my early headshots from my LA days, I barely had any makeup on at all. *All My Children* changed my life in many ways, and I've been a lover of long lashes since that first day in the makeup chair. All in all, there's a reason people love watching daytime soaps. You watch for so long that the characters start to feel like family. That's how it was for my mom and grandma. If you watch throughout your life, you grow with the characters. That's how I felt about it, too, as a little girl watching the show, and then as a part of it myself.

I was in a bad place after *All My Children* was canceled. I was lucky to be one of the cast members who was snatched up quickly when I booked an amazing guest role on *Body of Proof.* After that, it was a roller coaster of auditions and rejections for over a year. I started to think of myself as that girl who booked one job on a soap and then disappeared forever. I felt like my agents and casting directors were losing interest in me, which was scary. I didn't allow myself to wallow forever, though, and instead took matters into my own hands. I decided to make a mood board.

I'd manifested my dream job by convincing myself I'd be on a soap, so the mood board served a similar purpose. I actually found it in storage recently, and some of the things I put on it are embarrassing, and if anyone had seen it at the time, they probably would have felt sad for me. But mood boards are supposed to be about your ultimate goals, right? No one makes a mediocre mood board. So I had images of a girl on a billboard, a picture of a shiny Emmy, a movie poster, real estate photos, and my dream car at the time, a BMW M6. Just so you don't think all I cared about were fancy cars and Emmys, I also had a side of the mood board that said "Gratitude," with images of everything I was grateful for, including my dog, friends, family, and a roof over my head.

Construction Tip

Never make a mediocre vision board.
This is not the place for photos of you being
sort of fabulous or one step below amazing.
Swing for the fences.

I don't feel like I have to prove myself anymore (well, not always), but at that time I felt like I had to prove myself *to myself*, and to all the people who had questioned me over the years. All careers are full of ups and downs. Another high point for me was getting a role on *Days of Our Lives* in 2013, but when my character was eventually cut from that soap well before my contract was up, I was devastated. Even so, I picked myself up, started thinking outside the box, and decided to try real estate. I figured you never know, maybe I'd end up with my own show on HGTV one day. I worked to get the license, I studied hard, and I blocked out any negativity or nay-saying. I had a feeling it was something I needed to do to be able to take charge of my own career, and nothing could have stopped me. The press likes to make it seem like people have "overnight success," or that things happen quickly in show business. None of this, not the soaps or *Selling Sunset*, could have happened overnight. Most people who have so-called overnight success have worked their asses off for years to get where they are.

About a year after I got my license, I got an email from a casting director about a Netflix show about LA real estate and the Oppenheim Group. I had met Jason Oppenheim at a party in LA, and he told the producers of the show about me. I met with the creator, Adam DiVello, who also created *The Hills*, and what was funny was that I thought the meeting was another audition process, but then and there I realized they were pitching me to be part of the show. So it goes without saying, I got the job. Was it because of my mood board? Because I believed so fiercely that this was my next step? There's no way to know, but I do know that I believe in manifesting your dreams and visualizing what you want for your future. I believe in doing everything you can to make that happen. Sometimes it takes creating insanely ambitious vision boards and listening to your inner voice, even if your inner voice is an off-key rendition of Whitney Houston's "I Will Always Love You."

A Kentucky Girl's Guide to Making It in the Big City

Living in New York and LA after a lifetime in small towns taught me a few things about surviving in a cutthroat, fast-paced world—and loving every minute of it. Here are a few things I learned along the way.

Don't go barking up the wrong tree. Don't wave at everyone you pass. You think you are being friendly, but in a big city it attracts the wrong attention.

You can put boots in the oven, but it don't make 'em biscuits. Sweetbreads are not sweet and are certainly not bread. Google is your friend when eating at fancy restaurants.

Hey y'all. Your accent is your superpower. You can lose it, but don't forget it. It can magically open many doors.

Hold your horses. Don't give people the benefit of the doubt if you don't know them. It seems like the nice, sweet thing to do, but do the opposite until you know their true intentions.

Bless her heart. Just because you live in a big city now, you don't have to lose your charm. It takes all kinds to make the world go 'round; try to keep your cool, but don't let them mistake your kindness for weakness.

Lost as last year's Easter egg. If you are used to directions including landmark oak trees, flagpoles, and Piggly Wigglies, it's going to be quite a shock. You will now have the benefit of GPS, which would have saved me many a lost afternoon had this been around a few years earlier.

Till the cows come home. Traffic is going to be a new concept to you, so give yourself twice the amount of time it should take to get anywhere.

Don't get too big for your britches. It's amazing to explore the world and see how other people live. But there is no place like home, and always remain grateful for the people who raised you and showed you what's really important.

CHAPTER FOUR

Up Your List Price

I'm not a great swimmer. I basically learned to swim when I was a camp counselor in my early twenties, from the kids I was supposed to be watching. To be fair, I don't think what I do is exactly swimming, but more like trying not to drown until I get to a safe spot. To this day, I don't go underwater without holding my nose, and I have never dived headfirst into water in my life. I'm terrified of the ocean and never get farther than chest deep in a pool. So why the hell was I willing to put my life on the line and risk total humiliation on national television by high diving into the water on a show called *Splash*? (It was originally called *Celebrity Splash*, but I think the name had to change because of the lack of celebrities willing to risk their lives on live TV.) To be candid, I knew it was a bad idea, but I needed the job.

When *All My Children* was canceled, I booked a guest star-ring role in prime-time TV on *Body of Proof,* which was excit-ing, but it took up less than a week of my time. I found myself without a steady job on the horizon and back to the grind of audition waiting rooms and daily rejection. Most careers have ebbs and flows, but acting has tsunamis, droughts, hurricanes, and barren deserts. It's tough to hold on to your sense of self-worth, let alone your bank account, when you're weathering those storms.

So during one of these ebbs, when I got a call from my manager saying that this diving show would give me over six figures even if I got kicked off first, I figured it was worth po-tentially plummeting to my death in front of millions. Plus, it's not like I had any other options at the time. When you grow up without money, you learn to hustle to keep yourself financially afloat. No matter who you are, not knowing where your next paycheck is coming from can be a terrifying feeling. I figured I'd get the money even if I chickened out and belly flopped into the water, so I agreed. The press rollout might remind certain casting directors about me, I'd get paid, and I would hopefully live to celebrate it all.

But I never got the chance to sink or swim. Back in 2013 when this happened, there was a literal beauty queen named Katherine Webb (Miss Alabama USA 2012) who actually did become an overnight sensation when audiences saw her on ESPN cheering her college football player boyfriend, quarterback A. J. McCarron. The ESPN announcers made a big deal out of her (I mean, she was and is gorgeous), so she became an instant celebrity. And guess what? The producers of *Splash* decided to drop me and cast Katherine Webb in my place overnight. Talk about a humbling experience.

What seemed like a rejection at the time was probably the universe looking out for me by keeping me on dry land. The show only went for one season, as it was riddled with injuries of contestants who actually knew how to dive to begin with. I likely would have had to put that $100K toward medical bills if I attempted to dive. Thankfully, within about a week of my embarrassing *Splash* rejection, I booked *Days of Our Lives*. Things like that are a good reminder that everything happens for a reason, because of course I would rather do *Days* than freaking live diving! After I screen-tested, the producers of the show actually offered me two roles and let me choose which one I preferred. I was thrilled, and I picked Jordan Ridgeway, the role that felt most different to my *AMC* character Amanda Dillon, to challenge myself. As loyal as soap fans can be, they don't mind when the same actor plays different roles on two different shows. They actually seem to like seeing a familiar face. If an actor played two roles on the same show it gets a little trickier, but going from Amanda to Jordan wasn't an issue. It was such a relief once I booked that job. It was a lifeline that I desperately needed in that moment, because it made me feel that I was still viable, and that I was good at what I did. That's the thing though. Feeling viable shouldn't come from how much you're earning or how other people make you feel or whether or not you get to pike dive into a pool for money. It should come from one place only: you.

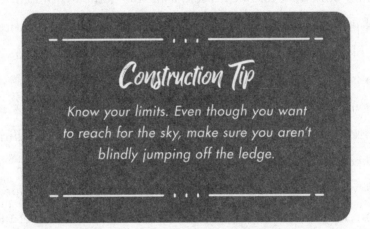

Construction Tip

Know your limits. Even though you want to reach for the sky, make sure you aren't blindly jumping off the ledge.

That's not an easy lesson to learn, but it's a journey I've been on pretty much my whole life. I remember my dad constantly getting screwed and taken advantage of by bosses when he was a mechanic, but he kept his head down (or under the truck hood) because he didn't want to lose the job, or the money.

My mom, like I've said, was more of a hothead at times, and she had no problem telling off a boss if she detected BS or felt she was being treated unfairly. I think I'm a perfect blend of my mom's and dad's attitudes. I can be fiery and stick up for myself, but at the end of the day I want to be a team player and I don't want to lose a deal or a job. However, sometimes it does get to the point where you have to be okay walking away. For example, when you're negotiating a contract or a salary at a job, and you truly feel like they're not valuing you. It's not about ego, it's about worth. I don't believe in asking for more because you feel entitled. It's more about your value, and what you're bringing to the table. And again, when I say *worth*, I don't mean money. For instance, on the same day I was interviewed for *Forbes* about my career successes, I went straight to the hellscape known as the DMV and sat in line for hours because I had to get a new license. After such a career high, there I was explaining to the less-than-thrilled DMV employee that my marriage didn't work out and I needed to change my name. No matter how much money or success you have, you still have to go to the DMV, wait your turn, and take a hideous photo for your license. At least I think everyone does this? Maybe JLo has someone go to the DMV *for* her, but "above standing in the DMV line" is a level of success very few of us attain.

Construction Tip

Stay humble, folks.

When emotions come into play, it makes it a little bit harder to figure out whether or not you should walk away from a situation. It's the same with homes. When I see people have an emotional reaction to a house I'm showing them, I know it's going to be tougher for them to negotiate. If you know you'll feel devastated if you walk away, you should probably rethink your plan. I've only walked away from contracts (on jobs or houses) if I was sure I'd be able to sleep at night. You need to assess what it's worth to you, and what *you're* worth, before you decide whether or not walking away is the right move. Unless you are into gambling, but I am not.

Like I said, figuring this out has been a journey. I didn't always have a choice, since I didn't have a family that could swoop in and pay my bills. I had to be financially independent, and that gives me a sense of pride. It makes me feel good to be able to help others and take care of myself. In my early days, it wasn't about me trying to up my price just to say I could; it was more like, *I need to figure this out to pay my bills.* As a woman in any field, especially in a profession where age is a major factor, it can get tough. There's a whole new level of anxiety that comes from being thirty-eight instead of twenty-two. In the television industry, it used to be that as a woman, once you hit about thirty-five your opportunities were numbered, but things are changing. Having hit a career high at the age of forty, I love that women are not only breaking the rules but also starting to make them.

It's still unpredictable, though. When I was on *Days*, I was working a job I loved, I had a story line I adored, and I had just filmed scenes that would lead to my first Daytime Emmy nomination. The day the executive producer asked me to his office, right after I filmed those scenes, I was on a creative and career high. The scenes were emotionally exhausting, but I was so happy knowing they went so well. I certainly wasn't prepared for what came next. The producer told me that new writers were coming on the show, and my character was cut (aka "moving to New York"). There I was, well before my contract was up, fired. Just another reminder never to get too comfortable, because the second you take one step forward, life might knock you two steps back. The key is to learn how to turn those steps into a cha-cha (even though that was the dance that eventually got me kicked off *Dancing with the Stars*). I didn't see any point in fighting back when I was cut, because they had told me in a respectful way, and I had learned not to burn any bridges. I had seen other actors try to fight things like that and it always backfired, so I thanked them for their time and moved on. I think because of that, they brought me back to the show several times. I also didn't push back because I don't want to be anywhere I'm not wanted. It's the same with relationships. I'm not going to beg someone to change their mind. I'd rather go somewhere I am wanted, and appreciated.

Within a month of getting fired, I decided to take some control of my future income and get my real estate license. I didn't want to feel passive forever, like I would have to sit around waiting for a call saying I landed a role, and a paycheck. Not that real estate is an easy payday. It's hard work—it can be incredibly stressful, and, yep, unpredictable. But it was another way for me to take care of myself, and my family. I chose real estate because I started thinking about other career paths I could take, and I wanted something more stable than acting, with more longevity. I wanted to be my own boss and not have my paychecks depend on the opinions or whims of a casting agent or a team of writers. Basically, I wanted something that would give me more control over my finances and security. I was also thinking in the back of my mind that hosting something on HGTV as a Realtor could be a good way to combine my two careers. Spoiler alert: it was.

When I was starting out in real estate, attending classes or holding open houses, there would be people who said things like, "Aren't you Amanda from *All My Children?*" Or "Are you Jordan from *Days of Our Lives?* Why are you selling houses?" The worst question I would get was "Did you give up acting?" I would always put on a happy face and make the career pivot seem like no big deal, but I was also processing some shame and letting doubts creep into my mind. I *was* that girl from the soaps, so what *was* I doing selling houses? Those were the moments I reminded myself to buck up. It was my choice to be there, and it did get easier with time and became a decision I could be proud of. I didn't quit acting or stop going on auditions and going out for things; I just took on another career so I could provide for myself. I wasn't giving up; I was being resourceful.

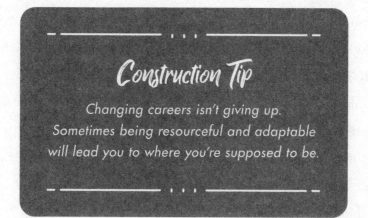

Construction Tip

*Changing careers isn't giving up.
Sometimes being resourceful and adaptable
will lead you to where you're supposed to be.*

I remember in 2018 when someone took a photo of the actor Geoffrey Owens working at a Trader Joe's in New Jersey, and the image went viral. He'd played Elvin on *The Cosby Show*, and there he was doing an honest day's work bagging groceries. The "job shaming" he endured caused a massive uproar, and people, including many actors, rallied to support him. I watched all this unfold, thinking of the judgment I had endured as well, and thought, *Hell yes!* Good for him for earning a living and doing what he needed to do. There's no shame in work, whether it's sacking groceries, fixing cars, working at Dairy Queen, or having a side career to supplement your passion. His story, and his reaction to it all, was so empowering, and it made me feel proud of my choice. He was so humble and unaffected by any negativity, and he stood by the fact that he was just making an honest living. He seemed so unfazed, and I loved that. I've never been someone who wanted to feel coddled and dependent. I've always wanted to work, and his story is a reminder that you are a badass if you are looking out for you and yours and doing what you need to do to get by. He went on to present at the Screen Actors Guild Awards after that "incident," and he ended up getting acting roles again, so you've got to love karma. I doubt the person who initially tried to shame him realized they'd be helping him get back in the game.

I felt proud of my decision to embark on a real estate career, but I didn't love the work immediately. At first I felt like a fish out of water, and I was starting at the bottom of the ladder, studying contracts and spending hours doing the tedious tasks that aren't glamorous or exciting enough to make good drama on a show. People see us on *Selling Sunset* and think, *I want to do luxury real estate!* Probably because it seems like you throw on some killer heels and a sexy dress and hang out in mansions until someone waltzes in to hand you a commission. It took me over a year to close my first deal, and that deal was actually representing my then fiancé in the purchase of his house. I always liked parts of real estate, but it was not love at first sight. My first sale was a cute home in the Valley in LA. It was a little over a million dollars, so small money by *Selling Sunset* standards, but it was a big deal for me. I was working with a guy who had more experience than I did at the time, but he took off to Thailand and basically left me to figure out contracts and negotiations. It was rough at first, but I got through it and made the deal.

Eventually I found my groove, first by helping friends and acquaintances find homes, and eventually branching out from there. I had experience before *Selling Sunset* happened, but even then I was the "new girl." I had to work my way into a tough, competitive environment, and although some, or several, tears were shed (more on that later), I always tried to keep my sense of self-worth, block out the haters, and do the job I was there to do. It was not always easy, and I admit the first season took me by surprise as far as how cutthroat some people could be, but I blocked out any negativity and stuck with it, and here we are.

Unlike so many professions where men tend to dominate (or act like they do), I think *Selling Sunset* is a pretty accurate reflection of how many women kick ass in real estate. I haven't had to deal with wage gaps there like I have in acting, especially during my early days in soaps, before the industry really started to take notice of the divide. When I was new to *All My Children*, a male costar was bragging about how much he made per script, and it was five times what I made. FIVE TIMES. Granted, he'd been on the show longer, but as I worked my way up, I never got close to his rate. I'm still not close to what he bragged to me about in 2005. I was excited for him since I'd just started, but it was an incredibly frustrating conversation to remember years later during contract negotiations. As a new actor I had no clue how to ask for more, and I wasn't comfortable negotiating or walking away from a deal to try to get more pay or better benefits. I had a "I'm just happy to be here" mentality that took me too long to get over. Yes, it's important to stay positive and be grateful for opportunities, but if you're working hard, it's also important to know when to fight for more.

But like I said, "worth" isn't always about money. Sometimes it's about your sense of pride or principles.

There are people who think the best way to prove your worth is to come in with guns blazing and cement your status as the loudest person in the room. That might work for some, but I've found that there's also a quiet kind of power, where you don't have to scream from the rooftops and bulldoze your way through life. I've learned to show my value by coming into new situations ready to sit back, listen, and learn—about the dynamics, the hierarchy, and who pulls the strings. Coming into new situations with respect for others, that is, not coming across as arrogant or egomaniacal, can go a long way. My tactic has always been to lie low and map out the landscape, and slowly decide whom I can trust and whom I can't. When I joined the Oppenheim Group and *Selling Sunset* started, I remember certain coworkers (take your guess) instantly trying to befriend me, telling me all kinds of gossip, and trying to turn me against people before I even really knew them. In life, instead of feeding into that short-term fulfillment, focus on the long game: yourself and the job you're there to do.

> ## Construction Tip
>
> If someone sits you down to give you the dish on a fellow coworker, unless that person is your ride-or-die, pretend that every conversation you're having is being recorded. Office gossip can and will be used against you.

By the time season two started, I felt like I'd hit my real estate groove, and I wasn't so green and unsure of myself. Real estate wasn't a side hustle anymore. I'd sold a few homes to people who were not friends, and that's when I realized, *Hey, this could actually work.* The more confident I felt, the more I enjoyed it, and the more confident buyers and other agents felt with me. If you don't believe in your own abilities, how can you inspire other people to give you a raise, hire you, or give you the job of your dreams? If someone or something is getting you down, whether it's in a job or at school or in your personal life, instead of wallowing for weeks, figure out what you can do to fix it. Can you take a class? Take the initiative on a new project? Find ways to make yourself an asset instead of letting yourself feel like a failure. One thing I've done with real estate is to mix buying and selling houses with charity events, so I'm bringing something unique to the process that's also positive, it gets the company press, and it shows them that I have a drive to shake things up a little. I did this on *Selling Sunset* when I threw a charity event at one of my listings. It was the night I auctioned off a coffee date with my ex-husband, who was a major star on a major TV show. The very next day was when I got a text saying he wanted a divorce. The charity event went amazing. The aftermath? Not so much. I hope that person got their coffee date, because to be honest I have no idea how that panned out. To that person, if you never got that coffee date, hit me up. The need to give back has always been with me. I know what it's like to go without, so whenever I can help others, I try to do my part. The point is, sometimes instead of sitting back and letting others decide your worth, you need to *show them* your worth. I try to do that by taking a unique or an unexpected approach to real estate.

Real estate, like acting or relationships, can be tough. Everyone has bad days, slow months, or disappointing years. It's not easy to rally and be your own cheerleader every second, and sometimes you just need to wallow for a minute. After that, though, you have to get back in the game and become your own hype man. Write down five positive things you bring to whatever situation is making you doubt your self-worth. I've done this after jobs didn't come my way, or things with work or relationships didn't go the way I planned. Think of new ways to tackle whatever is bringing you down. Part of your everyday job should be practicing self-advocacy. Put on Lizzo, Beyoncé, or Britney—whatever power anthem gets you off the couch, and remember your value. When I was doing *Dancing with the Stars*, I remembered that Beyoncé created Sasha Fierce, her alter ego that she could become onstage to embody her boldest, most fearless self. I'm forever inspired by Beyoncé, so I dreamed up my own sort of Sasha Fierce so I could go out onstage and let go of any doubt or negativity. It didn't turn me into the best dancer on the planet, but it helped.

How to Up Your List Price

I haven't mastered the art of upping my list price, but I have learned a few things over the years that help me feel confident, humble, and valuable at work. Here are a few tricks.

Find a solution to a problem. This is the basis for every great invention, from electricity to dip powder manicures. People who can solve problems instead of creating them (or solve the problems they create) are always valuable. Identifying a problem and then finding a solution will always get you noticed. There have been times in the office where Realtors will be getting into the weeds about a $2,000 HVAC repair, and risk losing a $5 million deal over it. I try to see the bigger picture, remind them that it's not worth losing the whole deal, and try to find compromises.

Have a side hustle. We all need to pay the bills, but so many hugely successful entrepreneurs started out working for nothing on a side hustle that they were passionate about. Your side hustle doesn't have to be some grand, complicated thing; it can be a simple passion that makes you feel good and supplements your finances or contributes to the greater good. Having something outside of work that doesn't take away from work will always add value to your life.

Think outside the box. You've heard this a thousand times before, and for good reason. Just because things are done a certain way does not mean it's the best way. Be tactful and don't try to change a whole work culture in a day, but if you get stuck in a rut, try to think sideways, upside down, or inside out. Shake up your approach. When I started at the Oppenheim Group, I went around to building sites in Los Angeles and gave them my materials and my card, which isn't standard practice. I needed a unique way to get my name out there, and I figured I didn't have anything to lose. I also love having fun with marketing materials, since luxury real estate can be a little stuffy. I moved to an area called Mount Olympus where the streets are called Zeus and Hercules, and so I marketed myself as the Aphrodite of Mount Olympus, as a way to stand out in a fun way. My two new escrows are showing that it's paid off.

Offer something unique. Have a special skill that can be incorporated into your work life? Think about ways to set yourself apart from the competition, whether it's something like a unique, eye-catching website or revamping your Instagram feed to show who you are and what you offer that's different (a sense of humor, a great personal style, etc.). In my opinion, the only thing worse than leaving a bad impression is not leaving one at all.

Take pride in your work. No matter what your current job is, or how far it is from your actual dream job, be the best at it. People take notice at all levels, and that work ethic will pay off.

Know your worth. People will constantly try to undercut your price because everyone is looking out for their own bottom line. If you're negotiating, be ready to back up your asks with examples and data to help drive home, without any doubt, the value you bring to the table.

Be a pleasure to work with. Just because you are doing well at work doesn't give you license to be a d*ck to others. People want a nice work environment, and this is an intangible asset that will come into play when decisions are being made.

Write checks your ass *can* cash. In business, I find it is better to underpromise and overdeliver. Always be realistic but hopeful. This helps get you a reputation as reliable and trustworthy, which is way better than being known as the one who is full of 💩 ;)

CHAPTER FIVE

Nice Girls Clap Back

All due respect to Michelle Obama, but every once in a while I find that taking the high road can be overrated.

Take Greg Chasen.

When I was a kid, this bully Greg Chasen, who tormented all the kids, came up to me and pulled my hair so hard he left a bald spot. An actual bald spot. I didn't pull Greg's hair in return or push him or even say a word to the guy. I just walked home with my sister, in tears. I'm not a fan of confrontation, plus I was in shock, so I guess you could call that taking the high road. When we got back and my mom saw my tears and my bald spot, she steered us off the high road real quick.

My mom put us in the car, asked me where Greg lived, and drove straight to his house. It was a small town, so every kid knew where every other kid lived. When we got there, my mom stomped up to the door and I hid in the car, ducking low so Greg wouldn't see me. I was horrified and had no idea what my mom was going to say or do. Greg's mom answered, and when my mom told her that he'd ripped my hair out, his mom didn't protest. I guess she knew her son could be a bully because she yelled, "Greg, get out here!" Scared of what was about to happen, I ducked even lower in the seat.

Greg walked out, and my mom *grabbed him by the hair*! He barely had more than a buzz cut, but still. Watching his legs kick as my mom picked him up by his hair was equal parts mortifying and thrilling. Parents would never get away with this now, but it was a different time, and a different town, and Greg's own mother wasn't even mad.

"Don't you ever touch my daughter again!" hissed my mom. In that moment there was no doubt that she meant business. So now Greg is crying, and I'm in a cold sweat. But I was also proud. Greg's mom just stood there, like, *See what you did, Greg?* After that, Greg never bothered me again, and I have my mom's willingness to confront a bully to thank for that. I'd like to think Michelle Obama would approve, but I'm not so sure.

I'm not naturally aggressive and I have a pretty long fuse, so it takes *a lot* to set me off. When I started at the Oppenheim Group, Christine Quinn was one of the agents who tried to befriend me at first, but she quickly turned into more of an antagonist than a buddy. She's beautiful, tall, and thin, and even though she tried to bond with me at first, I knew pretty quickly to keep my guard up around her, and I thought she possibly had ulterior motives. One minute she was inviting me to cocktails to give me the scoop on Hollywood Hills real estate, and the next she's using things I said out of context to pit me against my coworkers. We had a few on- (and off-) screen fights, and at first it was tough for me to keep my cool, but I did eventually learn to let her comments about me being "two-faced" or "pathetic" roll off my back, and I just kept showing up to do my job. You all have heard about the party that I wasn't invited to, where she created a drink called "Chrishell's Two-Faced Tonic." It was clear she needed to assert her dominance over the new girl on her turf, and she seems to enjoy hazing new Realtors.

I did leave a party one night at the end of the first season because I was so shocked by the level of antagonism. What ended up being a few minutes on a reality TV show in actuality was over an hour of what felt like public humiliation. I just needed to step away. Christine was laying into me about the fact that I had questioned Mary and Romain's relationship, even though I had already cleared things up with Mary and Romain. That was a turning point for me. I went home that night in tears, until I realized that that was *exactly* what Christine wanted. Me giving up, in tears. So I decided to hold my head up and never let anything she said or did get to me that way again. Life is too short to give some people the satisfaction of a single tear. After that night, I was done.

Despite my attempts to keep my cool, I did get nominated for an MTV Movie & TV Award for Best Fight for my rivalry with Christine on *Selling Sunset*, and it says a lot that when I heard about the nomination, I had no idea *which* fight they were talking about. Was it the explosive season one finale that ended with tears flowing and claws out? Was it the start of season three where we sat down to hash out all our issues? I'm pretty sure it was for our rivalry as a whole. It was no surprise that we lost to Kim and Kourtney Kardashian. Luckily, our fight wasn't physical like theirs was. Even though I do hate confrontation, I know when it's time to stand up for myself. You can't always be the nice girl. Sometimes you have to clap back by speaking up for yourself, ignoring someone when they're seeking attention (not easy to do), or politely declining an invitation that doesn't feel genuine to you.

When I do get upset, my heart rate revs, my nerves are shot, and my day is ruined. No matter what, though, you have to protect your own peace. If I do find myself getting upset, I take a breath and ask myself if it's worth it (that's where the long fuse comes in). The cliché "choose your battles" is a cliché for a reason. Constantly battling can be toxic. It's unhealthy. On the days we're not filming *Selling Sunset*, the vibe is definitely more casual. We might wear jeans or flats, and our hair and makeup aren't dialed up to a ten. It's still hectic, and we're busy making deals and going over contracts, but when the cameras roll, the drama does tend to heat up. No one wants to watch us quietly sign contracts for an hour. There are definitely some days I walk into the Oppenheim Group office and feel like I'm stepping into a hornets' nest, but instead of walking in ready to sting, I try to center myself, put on a power outfit, and walk in there equipped with solutions instead of drama. I'm not always 100 percent successful at this, but I do try. Our office is known for being very dog friendly, and sometimes those bitches are a lot nicer than we are.

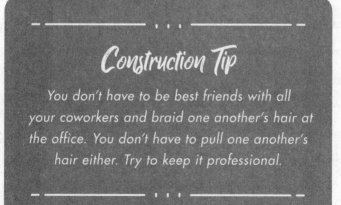

Construction Tip

You don't have to be best friends with all your coworkers and braid one another's hair at the office. You don't have to pull one another's hair either. Try to keep it professional.

People say it's bad to put up walls, but I'm actually an advocate for creating *healthy* boundaries, meaning protecting yourself by keeping your personal business and your emotions to yourself, if you know that showing them will cause someone else to use them against you. There is nothing wrong with feeling someone out before letting them in. Self-preservation is important, and over time I've learned to do this in my personal and professional lives. It doesn't mean you're not letting people in; it means you're only letting the right people in, and keeping toxic energy out. Like I said, I eventually figured out who my ride-or-dies were in the office. Going through a public divorce is a pretty quick way to find out, because you see who has your back and just wants to protect you, and who is dying to go in front of the cameras and do interviews about you.

I have grown really great relationships with so many of the agents at this point that they feel like family. Heather is the hopeless romantic who wouldn't hurt a fly (literally—she's vegan). Mary is the best friend and sister who always has your back, and she is one of the hardest-working people I know. Amanza is all heart, hilarious, and the life of the party. If and when she does show up, you know you're going to have a good time. Maya is an incredible mom and agent and her multitasking skills are seriously impressive. She also has a habit of saying the most hilarious things, and we joke that her Israeli accent seems to be getting thicker each day. Brett is like a brother to me. He'll tease you endlessly with love, I trust his opinion, and it's always a better time when he's around. And Jason . . . well, much more about that later. As for the agents who require a little more work, Davina is extremely direct, and that sometimes goes over well, and sometimes not so much. She's made a concerted effort to get along with everyone recently, and it has been much appreciated. Then there's Christine. At this point what can I say? She's beautiful, her ability to walk in seven-inch heels while pushing a stroller is very impressive, and her secret to applying the perfect red lip that never bleeds is something I've yet to figure out.

One key to being happy, especially when you're dealing with different personalities, is not letting things get under your skin, and if you keep out or brush off 99 percent of the negative interactions or relationships in your life, you won't be wasting energy and time on people or things that are just plain BAD for you. There are some everyday things you can't prevent, like people cutting you off in traffic or working with someone who has an agenda against you. I'm not saying to let these things go. I was raised by a mom who pulled Greg Chasen's crew cut, after all. But trying to be solution-based instead of reactionary is a tactic I always try to use. It usually takes someone making a very concerted effort to piss me off. I won't scream in your face, but I will likely go dead behind the eyes and freeze you out going forward.

Fighting doesn't always include hair pulling and punches and verbal assaults. Just like you can assert yourself with a quiet power instead of noise, you can shut someone down in ways that might not be obvious.

If there's anything I dislike more than confrontation, it's inauthenticity. On *Selling Sunset*, you have to watch your back, or else you could be metaphorically stabbed by a stiletto if you're not careful. After filming season one, Christine and I were left on horrible terms. We didn't speak at all, for months. Our interactions had given me so much anxiety that I put up a (healthy) wall, because it just wasn't worth my time or energy. So when we started filming again, we sat down and actually had a civilized, cordial conversation. I wouldn't say we were fast friends, but it was fine. Then about a week before her extravagant engagement party—the one with the live zebra wandering around—she said she was inviting me. I hadn't spoken to her in nearly a year, I'd met her fiancé once for maybe five minutes, and it felt weird to me to jump from that to suddenly being at her engagement celebration, pretending that nothing had happened. It felt fake and inauthentic, which is ironic, because I feel like she kept calling me fake. One minute we can barely be in the same room together, and now I'm on the guest list? It just felt awkward. She'd asked me to sit down and talk with her, and when she invited me to the party, right there to my face, I knew I had to tell her no. I said it in the nicest way I could, explaining that it would feel fake since we were barely on speaking terms. Even though I could tell she wasn't happy, I stood my ground on that decision.

Declining her invitation wasn't a clapback in terms of me trying to hurt her feelings. It was more about me creating a little peace bubble around myself, *for* myself. It was awkward to say no, but I felt it was the right thing to do, the genuine thing to do. At the end of the day, I think people appreciate it when you keep it real. I had to be up-front in that moment, and sometimes you have to do things that don't exactly feel good. It's like ripping off a Band-Aid. You have to suck it up and put on your big girl pants, and not do something that doesn't feel right to you just to make someone else feel better. But the fact that I didn't even hear about her engagement party until right before it was happening told me everything I needed to know. I wasn't about to just go for the sake of the show. I also didn't want to be lame and say yes and then flake. So this felt like the most honest way for me to handle it—not for anyone else, but for myself. Sure, I probably missed the only party I'll ever be invited to where a live zebra is a fellow guest, but I'm fine with that. I didn't accept her invitation, but I did send her flowers.

> ## Construction Tip
>
> You don't have to accept every invitation that comes your way, but it is always nice to send a gift. How nice that gift is can be totally up to you.

Although my office can at times be a hornets' nest, I've also met some ride-or-die friends whom I would do anything for. To me, ride-or-die means someone who won't just tell you what you want to hear; they'll be there through good and bad, with the truth. Sometimes you're popping champagne, and sometimes tears are flowing. Sometimes both at once. There's a quote I love that goes: "A good friend will bail you out of jail, but a true friend will be sitting next to you saying, 'Damn, that was fun!'" To me, that says it all. You want to hang on to the friends who'll stick by you during the worst times, and not just invite you to parties during the best.

It took me a while to find my ride-or-dies when I started at the Oppenheim Group. It's an intimidating group of powerful, successful women, and walking into that office as the new girl was a little scary at first, but I had to remind myself I'd done this before. If I had made it through soap diva initiation, I could survive real estate. On soaps, other actors might be suspicious that you're there to steal their spotlight, so I learned that it's best to come in humble (but confident), and not stride in there, guns blazing like you own the place. I had to do the same thing at the *Selling Sunset* office. I tried to walk in there with respect and establish that I was a team player, instead of a one-woman show. In both environments, people can get territorial or jealous, so even though I have a competitive edge, I had to quell all that drama and show them I was chill, I was there to work, and I wasn't there to try to ruffle feathers. It was rough in the beginning, but both environments reminded me not to take things personally. I've spent my entire life learning not to take things personally.

Some days can obviously be worse than others. If I need a little extra fire, I make sure to dress in something that makes me feel good about myself. Everyone has that power outfit that gives you a boost of confidence—one that's comfortable and doesn't require you to nervously fiddle with loose straps or an awkward collar. It may be a superficial fix, but it helps. That's something I learned in acting: when you put on the clothes, it helps you find the character. So when you're trying to bring out your inner Yoncé, dress the part. Whether it's a big interview, important presentation day, or you know you have to face a tough coworker, make sure you're not toddling in heels that are too tight or pulling on your hem. This was of particular importance on *Dancing with the Stars*. The week I was Maleficent, I kept having wardrobe malfunctions. We had to do a last-minute fix before I went onstage because it's tough to be a badass when your horns are flying off and you're tripping on your skirt.

You can pick outfits that inspire confidence, but you need to pair those outfits with some mental and emotional armor. When you set healthy boundaries, you're in charge of how much energy someone can suck from you. You're in control of your reactions, even though sometimes it doesn't feel that way. A boundary could be that you refuse to let a toxic person send you home in tears, or you could block them on social media, which might sound childish, but if it helps your mental well-being, I'm all for it. There have been plenty of days where I act tough at the office, but then go home and cry. I'm not an overly emotional person, but the learning curve was steep at times during the first season of *Selling Sunset*. It was such a stressful environment, and I had to remember to get in charge of my own energy, zip myself into my peace bubble, and create a force field around myself. There is power in saying, "I will never go home and cry about this person again." It might not always be easy, but saying it out loud helps.

I used to belong to the "never let them see you cry" club, but it's just not possible to hide your emotions all the time. Especially because if we film *Selling Sunset* for eight months, and if I cry two times during that whole period, that will be what ends up in the trailer, which I get because drama is more fun to watch than a bunch of people getting along all the time. If shedding a few tears helps you process your feelings in a healthy way, do what you need to do. I'm also a big advocate of therapy. I lost both of my parents and went through a painful divorce, all in a short time, so trust me, tears were shed. Crying can be a beneficial release. Everyone hits a wall at some point, and it's extremely healthy to talk about things that are upsetting or stressful, whether it's the loss of a parent or a conflict at work.

My therapist always says that when you do cry, don't wipe away the tears. Instead, pat them into your face. He is convinced they contain healthy, healing properties, which is a very LA thing to say. I'm a Kentucky girl at heart, so I skeptically googled it and couldn't find anything on it, so I'm not sure you can 100 percent rely on this advice. The sentiment is nice though. Don't be ashamed of those tears. Some other advice of his that's always stuck with me is not to let your self-worth be measured by outside opinions.

In Hollywood and in luxury real estate, I've found myself

opposite a certain type of man. He's always late. He's the most important person in a room full of important people. He's never, ever wrong. Ever. He's inconsiderate, rich, powerful, conceited, arrogant, rude, and condescending. I could go on, but you get the point. The way I bite back with these men is usually different from how I clap back with women. It goes along with that whole idea of power not needing to be loud. You don't have to bulldoze your way into a situation or scream and throw punches. You can be subtle. And this tactic is especially effective with this certain personality type. Not all men are the same, I know, but when dealing with this nails-on-a-chalkboard personality, I try to cater to their fragile egos. If I'm having an issue when I'm selling a house or buying a car or negotiating a contract, I've found that the easiest way to get what I want is to butter them up, as they say. Before you make your point, tell them how amazing they are at what they do. Say things like, "There's a reason you're at the top of your field," or, "Obviously you're brilliant and you know best, but . . ." Give their ego a fluff, and then, when they're vulnerable, step in with what you want or need or think. Lay the groundwork. "Your taste is impeccable, but the everyday person who isn't on your level might not appreciate the bespoke Vegas nightclub you turned your quiet Valley home into, so the stripper pole needs to go."

Construction Tip
Sometimes the best way to clap back
is to butter them up.

With women, it's more about showing respect. We're all different, obviously, so you have to read the room and understand
who you're dealing with. In general, I always try to make sure
a woman feels heard, because that's what we all want, right?
To be heard, listened to, respected? Some of the male trouble-
makers I deal with don't care about being listened to, they just
care about being "right." So with women, I validate their con-
cerns and listen. I'm not trying to divide all people into two
categories based on gender. I know we're all unique, and that
some women have fragile egos and some men want to go to
brunch and bond with you about business. I've just found tac-
tics that work when it comes to a certain kind of (nice) clapback, when you're trying to say no to something you believe is
unfair or unjust or wrong, and get your point across, not by raising your voice, but by using your smarts. I don't clap back often,

and honestly I don't usually have problems with people in general. Women have always been my key, core group. I've always bonded with feminine energy and been a girl's girl, as they say. It's very rare that I have a true rivalry with another person, but when it happens and the dismissive responses don't help, the best tactic is to IGNORE. Just walk away, get a cocktail, and hang out with someone else. However, if you happen to be contractually obligated to work with someone who inspires you to have homicidal fantasies about murder-by-stiletto, take a deep breath, laugh all the way to the bank, and maybe wear a block heel just to be safe.

Sometimes people see me as the "good girl next door" type, but if I'm pushed too far, my blood boils just like anyone else's. I feel like I'm a morally correct, good person, but that doesn't mean I don't want to wear something sexy or go dancing until two a.m. with friends. In my twenties I was always up for going out, but when I started *Selling Sunset* I was in a different stage of life. I was married and I might have dressed more conservatively or stayed in instead of dancing all night, but that's not the *only* way I am. I have a wild side and a crass sense of humor, believe it or not. What does any of this have to do with clapping back, you might be thinking? I guess it's just to say that at my core I am a nice girl, but don't make this southern belle rip off her tiara and yank you by your crew cut like my momma taught me.

Being nominated for an MTV award in 2021 for Best Fight is an honor I can absolutely promise you I never saw coming. I have learned that sometimes the fights that make you feel horrible—when someone has really gotten under your skin and made you feel like absolute crap—usually aren't as serious as they seem in the moment. With a little distance, you can see that something that felt so monumental doesn't matter in the whole scheme of things. If going dead behind the eyes or ignoring someone or catering to their fragile ego isn't working, my personal favorite tactic is humor. I always keep humor handy, as something to grab from my tool belt when I'm uncomfortable. You can be self-deprecating to break the ice or lighten the mood if you're not getting along with someone, especially when you share a one-room office. You can despise someone, but if you can agree on something that's funny, it'll remind you, just for a moment, that they're not your mortal enemy. When all else fails, you can laugh, and even if the laugh only lasts a few minutes, it's something.

Reacting or responding to nasty remarks has taken on a whole new dimension with social media. You can disarm the haters by turning a rude or hateful comment into a joke at their expense. It's sort of the virtual version of my mom pulling Greg Chasen's hair. I've dealt with my fair share of online bullies. Mostly I love interacting with people online, and their comments are positive, but every once in a while, I'll post a bikini photo or something, and there'll be those harsh, mean-spirited trolls who feel the need to reply with how much they loathe you and the fact that you breathe.

It happens.

On Earth Day 2021, for example, Instagram became littered with thirsty photos of scantily clad people posing in beautiful landscapes to show off the contours and curves of . . . our planet. Not one to take myself too seriously, it seemed like a fun trend, and hey, I was single. These ovaries aren't going to pollinate themselves. I was wearing a LaQuan Smith bodysuit on the beach, and I added the hashtag #thirstythursday. Maybe the image startled some people who just see me as that 2D "girl next door." One of those people actually felt the need to comment: *CHEAP AND SLUTTY!!!!!!* I was in on the joke, so I wasn't offended, but I could never stand by and let someone call LaQuan Smith cheap. I replied:

"Close. I can't accept that as an answer but I will accept expensive and slutty . . . that 💩 ain't cheap."

Anyway, that person didn't comment after that. So make the haters feel ridiculous, use humor, keep your cool, and walk away (or close the app). Everyone has experienced their fair share of dealing with online bullies, and ideally you take the high road by ignoring them. Every once in a while, though, you've got to meet bullies where they are. There are also bullies who are actually dangerous, like people who DM me telling me to kill myself, and those people should always be reported. There have been times I've looked at a string of old DMs from someone and realize they have been telling me all the different ways I should kill myself *for days*. If I call them out, maybe by posting their DMs, they either stop or, occasionally, write back, "OMG you responded thank you!" Sometimes they're looking for attention, and sometimes it's darker. Sometimes I do try to call them out. I'm not condoning violence or verbally punching below the belt, but you've got to stand up for yourself, especially in extreme (but not dangerous) cases. Was a random stranger calling my thirsty Earth Day Instagram photo "slutty" extreme? Definitely not, but I found a way to hit back with humor because it's key to be able to laugh at yourself in life. You can never be the butt of the joke if you're in on it.

In conclusion, don't let toxic people steal your energy. Brush things off when you can, but sometimes you need to recognize real boundaries you've set for yourself. I can have a laugh about someone making fun of my clothes or anything superficial. I can even laugh at myself about the ridiculousness of going through a public breakup via text. However, there is a line that healthy people recognize as being below the belt. Having to spend thousands of dollars in legal fees to kill false stories in the media that were blatantly untrue and intentionally hurtful is my own personal boundary. When I was pushed to sue for libel, I was told that the false stories were spread by a cast member, and I quickly came to my own conclusions about who that cast member was. Luckily I was able to prove that those false stories were untrue and keep them from being printed. Maybe your boundary is something different, but mine is attacking my character. Probably best not to attack my family or my dog either.

Classy Ways to Clap Back

Humor. Ever see a stand-up comic get heckled? It always ends badly for the heckler, hilariously for the audience, and as a win for the comic. If you are clever and quick on your feet, this can be an entertaining way to let people know not to mess with you.

Power moves. Cut your haters off at the pass. Sometimes you can refuse to work with them, and if you have the rank to pull this off, it will quickly prove they will get left behind if they don't play nice in the sandbox.

Kill them with kindness. Jealous and insecure people are the biggest bullies. If you are able to recognize this, it makes it easier to lay on the sweetness. Hurt people hurt people, as they say. Sometimes the best way to catch them off guard is to play nice. It shocks them and stops them in their tracks.

Go dead behind the eyes, all while smiling. If you're experiencing a conflict that will likely go away if you just smile and nod, like someone challenging you about whether the best decorating style is Spanish or Mediterranean, sometimes it's worth it to preserve your own energy and move along. The smile does not need to be convincing; it just needs to be present.

Social status. Want them to know you are thriving and not just surviving? Social media can come in handy for those amazing life updates and hot-girl-summer pics you know your haters will see. Being booked and unbothered might show people you're doing just fine, but it's not something that should be faked. If you are *actually* booked and unbothered, then post away. If you're pretending, that's probably not the best route to take.

The subtle drag. Sometimes you absolutely need to speak up, and if you do this while staying calm and sticking to facts, you can properly and succinctly drag someone to their place without ever raising a finger or voice.

Ignore. Every situation is different, but sometimes the fastest way to get bullies or trolls to move on is to not give them the reaction they were looking for—which means no reaction at all.

Success. The best clapback is the one that speaks for itself. As Taylor would say, "shake it off" and continue to rise. Let any doubters fuel your drive all the way to the top.

CHAPTER SIX

Just My Luck

I t wasn't luck that brought my sister Shonda and me a shiny black boom box with a double cassette deck that we used to blast New Kids on a loop. It was a shrewd business sense.

We were in middle school, and all the kids were in a competition where we'd go door-to-door selling items from a catalog to neighbors. Whoever sold the most candy and Christmas ornaments and holiday potpourri won the coveted boom box. Shonda and I teamed up, but the brother-and-sister team who lived next door made the mistake of bragging about how they had outsold us within a few days, so Shonda quickly devised a plan.

We wanted to win that prize, so Shonda talked the neighbors into giving us their sales points. In return, we promised them that we would give them our points the following year. As an adult it's easy to see that this deal was flawed, but as kids it seemed genius. We convinced them that this was a wise move on their part because it would ensure first place wins for the both of us two years in a row, but we would of course go first because it was our idea, and they agreed. Shonda's persuasion was brilliant, and we easily took home the top prize. The next year we followed through on our promise and gave the neighbors our points, but when you know the points aren't yours before you even start knocking on doors, it is kind of a motivation killer. That is the flaw we all missed. Our sales hit a slump the next year, and they didn't end up reaching the top spot, but at least bagged the second-place prize. Sorry, neighbors, I owe you a boom box!

Though not the most foolproof plan, Shonda's elementary negotiation was a good reminder that life isn't just about luck. It's about hustle, grit, and thinking outside the (boom) box. We definitely should have hit the pavement harder a year later to uphold our end of the bargain, but we were kids, and we definitely let them borrow our boom box a few times. Pretty early on in life I learned not to rely on luck, whatever that word means. Is it fate? Chance? Both? Does it mean that things come to you not because of talent or persistence or skill, but because the universe just happened to drop some good stuff in your lap? I'd rather believe good things come from hard work and determination than some fuzzy idea of luck.

> ## Construction Tip
>
> *Luck is what happens when preparation meets opportunity. No, I can't take credit for this definition—it was an ancient Roman philosopher named Seneca—but let's keep it real, I found it on Google.*

Growing up, my parents used the phrase "just my luck" constantly. There's an argument to be made that they didn't really have bad *luck*, but that they made some pretty bad choices, so a lot of things were bound to go wrong. For instance, getting a ticket for speeding with expired tags. They thought that the world was out to get them, and as two people who faced their own struggles and didn't have a ton of options growing up, in some ways maybe it was. After years of hearing my mom say, "Just my luck, we got a flat tire," or "Just my luck, our roof is leaking," it became a phrase I used quite often too. Whether it was when I was cast as Toto instead of Dorothy in the school play or when our house burned down, it became a go-to phrase. Once, after a bad day, I said, "Just my luck," and suddenly realized what I was actually saying. In that moment, having a "just my luck" attitude seemed depressing to me, as if you expected bad things to happen to you, and you felt cheated if things didn't go your way *just because they should*. I decided that I would never say that phrase again. I would never again assume that the world owed me anything. It was up to me to create my own luck.

Life has a way of knocking you on your ass when you least expect it, and so conditioning yourself to turn tragedies into triumphs is key. It's about having a victor mentality instead of a victim mentality. In many ways that's what this book is all about. I'm not saying it's easy to just snap your fingers and make believe a horrible experience is a good thing, but I am saying that you can teach yourself to see things in a differ- ent light over time. Sometimes it takes work, or therapy. Wine helps too. It's a commitment. People go through heavy shit. I've lost loved ones, gone through a divorce, lost out on jobs, and experienced a childhood that many would consider dan- gerous. Life can get tough, and sometimes it is more than you can handle. Three cheers for therapy. On a day-to-day basis, I've learned not to let the bad things inform how I live or who I am. Not many people have a totally charmed life 365 days a year, so try and identify the things that truly drag you down, heal from them, and move on. Maybe I have been in LA too long, but I really believe if you want your energy to be clear, not cloudy, it's up to you to do the work to bring the sunshine.

I'm a big believer in grit, which others might call chutzpah or backbone. It means you can dig deep and face the bad stuff, root yourself in the ground and not get pushed around. I used to be someone who was easily taken advantage of, whether that was by weird managers in Los Angeles who prey on young women heading to the big city with big dreams, or by bosses or ex-boyfriends. I feel like now, at forty, I am just starting to come into my own. I've learned not to accept things at face value, but to question them, and to assert my value, whether emotionally or financially or practically. I work on it every day and try to use the lessons from past experiences to make me stronger and remind myself that life isn't about luck. It's about perseverance. We're all works in progress, and I expect to be working on myself in some form for many years to come. Being in a constant state of construction isn't necessarily a bad thing, and each experience hopefully gets you closer to your redesign. I do not want to be making the same mistakes I made at twenty-five when I'm eighty-five!

All this tough love talk doesn't mean that you have to walk around choking back tears and emotion. Sometimes you need to fall apart for a little bit, but notice I said *a little bit*. There's a difference between getting into your feelings and straight up wallowing. Get in your feelings, but don't stay there. Have a good cry instead of sweeping your emotions underneath the rug. There's a difference between shutting yourself inside for a few days or weeks and letting the feelings flow after a painful breakup or the loss of a loved one and shutting yourself inside and wallowing because you didn't get invited to a party or you were passed up for that promotion. If the pain cuts deep, realize that you need to take care of yourself and figure out what you need to do to open the windows again and let in the sunshine. Get up, dress up, and show up. It's obviously a lot easier said than done, but swapping out your robe for some pants (ball gowns are not necessary) can go a long way. Have a friend over, or take your dog to a park. Start moving your body, and your mind will follow. It puts the plan in motion so you can start to heal.

This isn't just reserved for life-changing events. It can apply to everyday setbacks. I didn't rely on luck when I entered that all-male acting competition to get college scholarship money. Instead of saying, *Just my luck, it's for men,* I read the fine print, entered the damn contest, and won. My efforts don't always lead to a win, but if you're reading this book, you already know that. Several years ago I was actually supposed to be the next Bachelorette. It was all set to be announced! Then in season eleven of *The Bachelor,* when Brad Womack didn't pick either girl, DeAnna Pappas went on *Ellen* and talked about getting rejected by Brad, and Ellen declared that DeAnna should be the next Bachelorette. Fans rallied around, the network listened, and my announcement was pulled. I never got the chance to hand out that fateful rose. I was in my midtwenties at the time, and I was definitely bummed. Looking back now, I can see that everything happens for a reason because for so many years my love life wasn't the main topic of conversation, and if I had done *Tthe Bachelorette*, my love life would have been THE topic of conversation. My work and career are so important to me, so speaking as someone who ended up having their love life overshadow their career at times after all, I guess sometimes you can't escape your fate, and embracing it has become empowering. Instead of fighting against the fact that my love life has been torn apart and analyzed and misrepresented, I've learned to go with it, and speak up about things when I need to, but ignore the haters when it just doesn't matter.

Another potential "just my luck" moment happened in 2012, when I was supposed to be in a Nickelback video (I know, I know) with Jason Alexander, aka George Costanza from *Seinfeld*. I was thrilled to be cast. For context, this was just before so many people turned on Nickelback, and this video might have been the reason people turned on them. I was supposed to play the main dream girl, the object of Jason Alexander's love/lust, and I could not wait. Well, a few days before the shoot, I got a call from the director saying that an actress from *Baywatch* who supposedly knew the band was going to play the dream girl instead. I was devastated and felt totally defeated. In the video, Jason Alexander plays a barista who crushes on a gorgeous woman (insert *Baywatch* beauty here). He fumbles around with the cups and lids because she's just so hot, he fantasizes about her in a bikini on a raft as he makes her latte, and it just gets worse from there. Seriously, it's worth a google. When that video came out and I finally watched it, I realized that maybe my luck isn't all that bad because it was declared one of the worst music videos of all time. I guess I could have looked back and laughed at myself, but I'm okay not having gotten the opportunity to do so. There is no Nickelback video for my grandkids to watch and see me sexily rubbing coffee beans all over myself and say, *What the hell was Grandma thinking?*

Yet another big disappointment happened more recently, when I was cast in the Disney+ remake of *Cheaper by the Dozen* with Gabrielle Union and Zach Braff. I auditioned for a fun role and was told to hold the shoot dates, which meant it was down to me and maybe one or two other people. I was so excited about the idea of playing a mom opposite Gabby Union because I love her, and it seemed like such a big opportunity. Well, the phone rang, and . . . I GOT THE PART! I was super excited and immediately told my family and friends, which ended up being a mistake. I got another call three days later with the most clichéd Hollywood line, "We're so sorry, the network has decided to go in another direction for the role." I was down and disappointed, but by now I had been through this enough times that I know it's not about luck or my abilities or the universe being out to get me. It's the nature of my industry, which is real good at toughening you up. You can give your best and do your best, and you can get the job and lose the job within the space of a week. I don't sit around and cry about those so-called defeats anymore. Sure, I might mourn them with a glass of wine, but then I open the curtains, get up, get out, and do it all again.

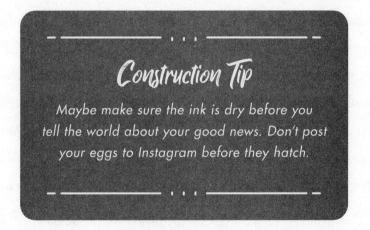

Construction Tip

Maybe make sure the ink is dry before you tell the world about your good news. Don't post your eggs to Instagram before they hatch.

Like I've said, it's not always so easy to pull yourself out of a funk and stop wallowing. Sometimes a situation merits some serious wallowing. After a battle with cancer, my mom passed away in July 2020. The world was stuck in the coronavirus lockdown, and I'd just suffered this tremendous loss. It was a terrible time, and you bet your ass I wallowed. Not long after my mom died, I got a call asking if I wanted to be on *Dancing with the Stars*. It seemed like the exact opposite activity you would want to do in the midst of grieving, but I *knew* my mom would have wanted me to do the show. She had always loved dancing, and some of my favorite memories growing up are of us dancing in the living room or at my dad's live shows. It suddenly felt like the perfect way to push myself to get up, dress up, and show up.

In the beginning, I felt unsure about everything, like nothing I was doing felt right. But it didn't take long for me to feel like dancing was the exact right thing to be doing, even if my scores didn't reflect that. Looking back I wouldn't trade that experience for anything. I felt my mom with me the whole time, especially on the night I shared my story about my parents and was able to dedicate the dance to them. Doing *Dancing with the Stars* took me from victim to victor real quick and helped me channel my grief and the love I felt for my mom and dad (who had passed shortly before) into art. It gave a purpose to the pain that told me I was exactly where I was supposed to be. I was in the middle of freezing my eggs when I did that show (more on that later), I'd recently gone through a divorce, and I'd lost both of my parents, but I was still willing to make an ass of myself doing the cha-cha. It was terrifying and exhilarating, and it had nothing to do with luck. It was about learning each step, getting up after falling down, trying to point my toes even when my feet rebelled, and accepting the results rather than saying, "Just my luck."

I love that moment of pride when you get through something that absolutely terrifies you. When I was asked to dance on live TV, I didn't dive in right away (because remember, I can't dive). There was definitely hesitation because I am NOT a natural dancer. But it's nice to be asked to the party, even if you're scared that you'll be the first one who gets kicked out. Facing a fear is part of the challenge. It was an eight-week journey during one of the most difficult times in my life. I started at the bottom, I learned the steps, I felt all the feelings and then let them go. I didn't worry about my luck or blame my luck or believe that luck had anything to do with it. All I did was say yes. And then I danced.

CHAPTER SEVEN

Not So Cinderella

I've never been the best at picking men, which, if you know anything about my love life, might sound like an understatement. I had plenty of preteen crushes, like Jonathan Taylor Thomas (JTT), Jordan Knight, the Karate Kid (aka Ralph Macchio), and don't judge me, but Scott Baio from *Charles in Charge*. He wasn't political back then, and he was hot! Or at least, I thought he was hot when I watched him on TV back in Kentucky.

It's safe to say that I was boy crazy from a young age. I remember a kid named Brandon Hooker in elementary school printing me a heart off an ancient printer, the kind with the perforated paper. If you don't know what I'm talking about, you're probably way younger than I am. If you do, welcome to your forties. I was so excited about the paper heart that I ended up doodling *Terrina Chrishell Hooker* all over it. But the next day, Brandon printed out a paper rose for Heidi Johnson, which I guess was my first brush with ghosting. After that failed almost-romance, it was me and JTT and the Karate Kid for most of my early years. I would develop crushes on boys, the kind where they take up all your brain space and you gaze at them lovingly across the classroom, but it was all unrequited.

Then I met Jace.

I was a sophomore in high school with major insecurities, and he was the kind of kid who seemed cool and confident. Despite my insecurities, I was a straight-A student, and he was a stoner who liked to start fights and cut class. His bad-boy image gave me a chance to rebel, and I was drawn to him like Elvis to sequins. I would have done anything for Jace. In this case, "anything" includes getting patted down to visit him in the county jail when he was busted for selling weed. I got good grades and studied hard, but I gravitated toward the stoner kids because, well, they were the ones who were nice to me. They weren't overly concerned with money or status or what car you drove. It was just about having fun, and being cool to one another. Jace was part of that group, and I fell fast and hard for him even though his only redeeming qualities were that he liked me back and we lived in the same town. And yes, he had that bad-boy thing going on.

We dated for most of high school, until I found out he'd been cheating on me and sleeping with a redhead in our school. At the time I was devastated, and it didn't help that they welcomed a cute ginger-headed bundle of joy a few months later. I was willing to sacrifice everything for Jace, to my detriment. It's a pattern that I have repeated over the years, but it's tough to be practical about love when you're a hopeless romantic. Just remember the adage, "Life is not a fairy tale; if you lose your shoe at midnight, you're drunk." I spent a long time looking for my prince, and now I know to look past the show-off and go for the stable, sweet guy. Now instead of being lured by six-pack abs, I'm way more turned on by compassion and consistency. If they also recycle and love animals, they may as well be Brad Pitt.

In college I actually did fall for a sweet, nice guy. I'll call him Alex. He was a drummer in a local band and my friend was dating the guitar player, and I met Alex one night at a show. Later he ended up bonding with my dad over music, and I loved that he treated his own mom like gold. Alex was good to me and just an all-around solid guy. He drove out to Los Angeles with me after we graduated and tried to live there, but he wanted a small-town life with a wife and kids, and I was nowhere near ready for that. So I guess I was the one who was unable to commit at that time, because I decided to stay in California and pursue my career. At my core I'm a city girl, so we just wanted very different things. We were so young, and I had to put myself first if I was going to accomplish all I'd set out to do. I couldn't be held back, and that was the first time I realized I had a say, too, and I didn't just exist to please a man. My value wasn't based on how much a guy liked me. After a few months of trying to make it work, Alex went back home. We were both sad, but we also both ended up pursuing the lives we wanted. I actually ran into his dad in Kentucky a few years ago while visiting home, and it was nice to hear that he was doing well. Timing is everything, and even though Alex was a great guy, our timing was way off.

I feel like I have pretty good intuition about people in general, but with men, history has proven I have a massive blind spot for red flags. In the past when confronted with a very obvious red flag, I've tended to ignore or rationalize it. The biggest problem is that I have a history of falling for what I'll call love bombers. They're the ones who shower you with affection from the moment you meet; they constantly tell you how they've never felt this way before, that you're the most gorgeous human on the planet, and their world doesn't turn without you. You are THE ONE. They bomb you with praise and devotion so intense that you get so caught up in the romance of it all and you miss the bright red flags slapping you in the face. It's a smoke-and-mirrors tactic, and it's pretty effective, I hate to say. Their sweet nothings end up being just that—nothing. Because as fast as the flame of their love starts burning, it dies out just as quickly. They pour all the gas on the fire, and after it burns off, you are left with the ashes and heartbreak, all while watching them burn for the next unsuspecting girl (who is now excitedly telling all her friends how her new man told her she is THE ONE). In love, the math tends to get fuzzy. Sometimes THE ONE plus THE ONE equals The Third Wheel.

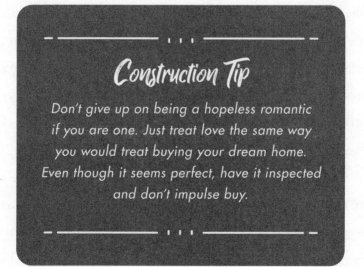

Construction Tip

Don't give up on being a hopeless romantic if you are one. Just treat love the same way you would treat buying your dream home. Even though it seems perfect, have it inspected and don't impulse buy.

I am still a work in progress when it comes to relationships, but I like to think I have learned a little bit over the years. I have a history of going for similar types, like actors and performers who are super passionate about everything, including me. At least at first. As reluctant as I am to talk about my exes in depth or to criticize anyone I've been linked to, most of it has been in the tabloids at some point, so I guess this is my chance to tell my side of the story. I'm thankful for where I am, as painful as some of my breakups may have been. I dated *Glee* actor Matthew Morrison in my midtwenties, and we fell in love and got engaged. I was a small-town girl, and this was my first adult relationship. I didn't fully understand what a healthy, solid relationship looked like, even though of course I *thought* I did. If you've seen *Selling Sunset*, you might know how that relationship ended because during one of the on-camera interviews I said, "If I ended up with the person I was with when I was twenty-five, I would want to kill myself . . . Yeah, you can google that. You were a d*ck! Sorry!" I try to preserve my privacy, but sometimes a girl has to tell it like it is, I guess.

A lot of time has passed since that relationship ended, and we can both laugh about it all now. It's not like we're hanging out and bonding every week, but we've run into each other a few times over the years and even though I sounded a little

angry on *Selling Sunset*, it's always cordial. He's said in interviews that he felt pressure to get married at that time, not from
me, but from society. Looking back I know it never would have
worked out, and we were so young and we each still had a lot
to learn. Not that I'm making excuses for him, but I'm just
glad, in retrospect, that it didn't work out.

And then there was Justin, whom I met in 2013. I knew
of him just from being in the soap world. He had been on
Passions and I was on *Days of Our Lives* at the time, and a
mutual friend introduced us. We hit it off right away and were
pretty much inseparable from day one. I fell hard and fast and
thought that he hung the moon. He proposed in 2016, and we
got married the next year. And I, like most everyone who gets
married, thought that was it.

In 2019, while I was filming *Selling Sunset*, he filed for divorce and notified me via text. Although there were definitely
signs that things were far from perfect, ending things in such
a finite way, without talking it through with each other or
friends and family, was a complete shock. I was devastated,
of course. The night before, I'd been hosting a charity event
where he donated some signed items to be auctioned, and the
next morning, it was all over. The last thing I want to do is
rehash old wounds, but being so far away from it now I can see
that what happened was a gift. Now I understand much more

clearly how I deserve to be treated. You can be completely in love and then find yourself reeling from a breakup, but you can also move on with your life, realize that it was definitely not meant to be, and find something, and someone, so much better. It takes time, but it can, and will, happen.

More than once, I swore I would not let my love life become tabloid fodder again, but you can see how well that turned out. Something takes over when you fall in love. You feel secure and so sure of the relationship that you want to scream about your love from the rooftops. This is usually the phase where people decide to get someone's name tattooed on their body with some questionable ink. I've made some bad decisions about tattoos (getting one from a drunk tattoo artist? Guilty.), but luckily a tattoo of someone's name is not one.

When someone is in love, it's hard to convince that person that the relationship isn't right, which is why oftentimes friends only speak up once in the beginning or not at all. Even if he's waving red flags like a bullfighter to everyone around you, you're the girl striding right up to him, oblivious to any impending danger. Everyone around you is screaming and waving their arms because they know it's not going to end well, but you're too distracted and in your own world to listen. But also, sometimes a healthy relationship that starts out with zero warning signs can turn toxic over time, and you can end up bringing out the worst in each other simply because it wasn't meant to be. In other words, *it's complicated*. If you're a naturally optimistic person like I am, it's hard to look for warning signs when you're falling in love. You're hopeful, and no one's perfect, and everything in you wants it to work. As a matter of fact, my blood type is B+. So it's literally in my blood to BE POSITIVE. With that rationale, some (me) could argue that my blood type has also been BE STUPID, but I digress.

When I got married, I imagined being eighty years old on a porch with my husband someday, holding wrinkly hands and laughing about an inside joke. I fell fast and hard. I didn't mind my love life being public, because it was something I was so proud of. I always wanted to have a family, and at the time I thought I was with the love of my life. So of course I was happy to share that. However, I never could have predicted how it all came crashing down so forcefully. Divorce is humiliating, and it can make you feel like a failure as a person. Now add tabloids, paparazzi, and a camera crew following you in real time, and it was a recipe for the lowest point in my life to date.

I have been asked so many times why or how I continued to film *Selling Sunset* through it all. Of course, after receiving the infamous text that my now ex-husband had filed for divorce, I contemplated quitting. I contemplated quitting a lot of things because suddenly I felt like nothing mattered, including myself. I had put so much of my identity into that relationship that I no longer knew who I was without it. It took some convincing on the part of the producers to make sure I knew that the show was not looking to exploit my pain, but instead would allow me to share my story on my own terms. I had just lost my dad that year, and now I was losing my husband and best friend, my teenage stepdaughter whom I no longer see but who still has a huge piece of my heart, and many of the friends who were his friends before we met. I ultimately decided I couldn't lose my job too. In a way, it was all I had left. It was a second career that I had worked really hard for, and I was not willing to give up on it. Even though I was unsure how I would actually get through it, I had to try. I felt like a shell of myself, but there was comfort in knowing the show had to go on, and so did I. I still wonder why he wouldn't have wanted to separate in private and wait to file for divorce a month later when *Selling Sunset* would be finished filming, but what's done is done. I was terrified to put all that on camera, but I also trusted my producers and knew they would handle things with sensitivity. Nothing was exaggerated. It was horrible, and because it happened while I was in the middle of filming *a reality show*, it's forever out there for the world to see.

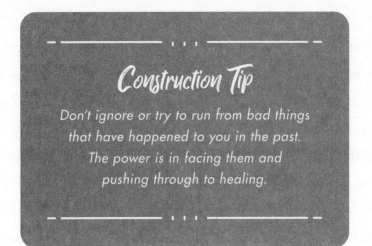

Construction Tip

*Don't ignore or try to run from bad things
that have happened to you in the past.
The power is in facing them and
pushing through to healing.*

I had a tremendous amount of anxiety before that season pre-
miered. My stomach was always in knots, I couldn't sleep, and
my hands would shake. I had no idea what the response would
be, but knowing the world was about to see me in my most
vulnerable state felt like impending doom. But then something
beautiful happened. Instead of receiving the hate I was expecting for such a messy public divorce, I received the opposite.
People started sharing their personal stories with me online and
in hundreds of Instagram DMs a day. This was right in the
middle of the Covid lockdown, so I was overwhelmed, but I had
the time to read many of them. After going through something
so painful, and experiencing so much loss in one year, getting
that support, connecting with strangers in the middle of a pandemic, and being able to have a voice was ultimately healing.

There were several months between filming and the season premiere on Netflix. I used that time to heal and did a lot of work on myself through therapy and self-reflection. Part of adulting is realizing that there are two people in a relationship and owning your part in what went wrong. Being the victim and staying bitter won't help you grow and move on. Getting some distance from a relationship that you *think* is good for you allows you to see the cracks in the foundation, and to spot all the red flags. Of course, there were great things about our relationship at first, and for many years, otherwise I wouldn't have married the guy. Sometimes it's not easy to understand how unhealthy or unequal something is when you're too close to it, and when you're so in love. It's not just about identifying the things the other person did wrong, it's about looking at yourself, honestly, and understanding how choices you've made or ways that you've responded to situations might be unhealthy too. I made choices where I continued to date the same "type," even though those types tended to not be a good fit for me. I let things slide when I shouldn't have and didn't pay close enough attention to early warning signs. The closure comes from knowing that the relationship was not right for either one of us for different reasons. And although I wouldn't have ever handled the breakup in the way he did, I would have wasted a lot of time trying to fix something that was irreparably broken if we'd stayed together.

Did I learn from my mistakes after Justin? Well, like I said, when it comes to love I'm still a work in progress. I did fall for another love bomber not long after my divorce, and we were quickly heading toward real commitment. He was a tall dancer, and he started off as this amazing, positive, generous guy. I took him home for Christmas to meet my family. After the honeymoon phase, though, things took a turn. This time, instead of making excuses for his behavior, I actually opened my eyes, pushed past the smoke and mirrors, and saw the truth. I'd gotten stronger, and as soon as I realized how deep his apparent lies went, I was the one who ended it. While it hurt, I was able to put it all behind me quickly. Before him, after a breakup I usually couldn't eat or sleep, but this time was much different. I took care of myself, I kept busy, and I felt strong knowing that I'd done the right thing for me. I wasn't the clueless damsel in the horror movie. I turned around, faced reality, and got the hell out of the woods. Instead of feeling sorry for myself after we broke up, I felt empowered.

In between relationships, I go on dates like everyone else. Some good, some not so good. I've gone out with musicians, actors, businessmen, and everything in between. On every date you're looking to find some magic, which might be why I even once actually went on a date with a professional magician. Reader, let me assure you, there was no magic.

I met the magician, let's call him Harry, at a charity event one night. We were at the same table and he seemed like a nice guy, but what I really liked about him was that he was so passionate about what he did. Yes, he was passionate about *magic*, but I think it's sexy to love what you do, even if it involves card tricks and literal smoke and mirrors. On the night of our date he picked me up in one of those showy sports cars you have to practically dislocate a shoulder to get into. We were at dinner and it was by no means amazing, but it was at least okay. I told him I'd read an interview he'd done and that I loved that he was so passionate about his work.

"Oh, that's just a character I play," he said. What a buzz-kill. He said his love for magic was all fake, and that he just put on an act because it was better for his brand. The date got worse from there, and he turned out to be like the boys on the playground who throw sand in your eyes to show that they like you. He'd say charming things like, "Is that the only thing you could find to wear?" Was this guy for real? It was hard to tell if he just had a terrible sense of humor or if he was a true d*ck. I'm going with both. At some point during the night he asked how I thought the date was going, and put on the spot, I decided to be honest. So I told him I thought we had brother-and-sister chemistry, like he was going to give me a friendly punch in the arm or something. Immediately after I said that, he grabbed me by the back of the neck, pulled me to him, stuck his not-so-magic tongue down my throat, and in a horrific voice said, "Do I seem like your brother now?" I nearly dry heaved, and as you can probably guess, we never went on another date. I've added magicians to my list of red flags because of this guy, which I know is a stereotype, but come on. I'm still traumatized from the date. It's too bad we can't have Yelp reviews for dates.

Against my better judgment, I've also dated men who are younger than me. Not so long ago I had dinner with a guy who was, yes, in entertainment. He was also incredibly hot, and too young, but I'm human so I couldn't say no. The night went well, until the red flags started popping up—and this time I paid attention. He started saying things like, "I wonder what your fans would say if they knew we were together," which is weird because we were not together and because it's just a strange thing to say. Was he already plotting how many likes he'd get on Instagram if he posted a photo of us snuggling? We shared a very PG kiss at the end of the date—until he stuck his finger down my throat, which is a move that I guess was supposed to be sexy, but which for me was the opposite. He was too young and too hungry for attention, and then there was that throat jab, so we never went out again. I was perfectly fine going home to my cozy couch with my dog and a glass of wine.

Part of being a hopeless romantic is making sure that, no matter how hard things get, you don't carry bitterness around in your heart. You don't shut down and become cynical. I think I'll always fight to stay hopeful and to put my best energy into the world. I know there are amazing men out there, like my brother-in-law Chris, who always puts his family first and who loves my sister Shonda unconditionally. They've been together twenty-one years, they've raised three kids, and they've stuck together through all the ups and downs that life can bring. I'll give full credit to my therapist for something I said during season three of *Selling Sunset*, which was, "You don't just go out looking for greener grass; sometimes you have to water the grass you have." I love that, and it definitely resonated with me when I was going through my divorce. Without that attitude, relationships are much like car leases: traded in when the new model comes out. That's a fine way to treat a hatchback or an SUV, but not a partner.

Now, as I'm writing this book, I've been dating Jason, as in Jason Oppenheim, my "boss" on *Selling Sunset*. The news (since I guess my love life is news) broke in the summer of 2021, when we were on a trip to Italy and Greece with some other cast members and friends. We had been hiding our relationship successfully for quite a while, but I could feel that the walls were closing in. Several times, we barely escaped getting caught by paparazzi, and we were starting to see posts on pop culture Instagram accounts like Deuxmoi speculating that something was going on between us. We were in love in Italy and we got tired of hiding like two kids smoking in the bathroom, so we posted about it ourselves.

The internet melted when we let the world in on our secret, probably because it seemed like a curveball. Well, it was exactly that for us too. There was nothing romantic between Jason and me for the longest time. We were definitely not each other's types, and we had seen the best and worst of each other over the years. But one thing that never changed is that I was always completely myself around him. Through working with him every day, I developed a huge amount of respect for him. I always valued his opinion and his integrity. Over time, a core group of us from the office became extremely close, and we're either together at the office or together blowing off steam after the office. Jason was there for every breakup I had, and every bad day, and we became close through all those conversations. He became my best friend. I also never tried to impress him, except maybe for closing deals at work to prove I had the chops. I was just a goofball around him, because he was just my close friend Jason.

Talking to Jason became comfortable and comforting, especially in the middle of the craziness we found ourselves in with *Selling Sunset*. He usually dated twentysomething models and I always dated guys who were over six feet tall, so the thought of us being together didn't cross our minds. We used to commiserate about our respective breakups, like him with his latest gorgeous young blonde and me during my crash-and-burn with a very tall dancer. When we went out, I was an excellent wingwoman for him, helping him meet people, and he would do the same for me. Afterward, we would laugh about our respective bad dates and tell each other every detail about what went on. We didn't hold back with each other. That's how comfortable it was.

We would ask each other for advice about people we were going out with, and the bar got so high for both of us that no one was making the cut for either of us! Then one night when we were out, we kissed. What could have ended up with us laughing and saying *What were we thinking?* instead kicked off my first relationship where I've felt like I can be 100 percent myself, with my best friend. At this point I don't know what the future holds for either of us, and by the time you read this I guess we'll find out. One thing I am sure of is that we will always have an enormous amount of love, respect, and friendship between us.

No matter what happens, I know I'll be perfectly happy on my own, living in my dream home that I bought by myself, and decorating my glam closet exactly the way I want to. The most important thing in life is to focus on being a whole, happy person on your own, without depending on the attention of another person to make you feel fulfilled. Love and relationships don't get easier, but if you work at them, and work on yourself, you do get stronger. Just watch out for love bombers and people who have a strained relationship with the truth. Stay hopeful that there is someone out there who, when they say *I love you*, will mean it, forever. Until that person comes along, you might just have to be kissed by a few frogs (or magicians who jab their tongues down your throat) before you find the one.

If Men Were Houses

*Please note this is written from my point of view but can be applied to any gender or heart that gets your heart pumping.

The Fixer-Upper: They have a smelly roommate, and you can't be sure the last time their sheets were washed. Their clothes leave much to be desired, but they are a quality human who treats their friends, mom, and dog like gold. If you have the time/eggs for this, it can be a nice option.

The Flip: They aren't that experienced, and you are going to pour years into teaching them how to be considerate and what is and isn't acceptable behavior, only to have it benefit their next relationship. Once you realize this, don't worry about how much time you've already spent. Time to liquidate, it's pointless.

The Teardown: Run. I don't care if they're the hottest thing you've ever seen. I don't care if you've never felt passion like this with anyone else. Inspections came back with serious damage. You found out they're a serial cheater, a pathological liar, and their favorite topic of discussion is themselves. It may look good on the outside, but this house has major foundational problems.

The Airbnb: It's exciting and fun but not the place for long-term arrangements. When they tell you they aren't looking for a relationship, believe them! Maybe the conversation leaves much to be desired, but your chemistry in the bedroom is electric. Have a hot girl summer and enjoy! Just remember it's safe to get in the pool, not in your feelings.

The Dream Home: We're all on the hunt for these keepers, but they do exist. Like all the dream homes I have found for my clients and myself, they weren't necessarily what you expected but were the perfect fit in the end. Someone who will grow with you, encourage you, and be secure and happy with who they are. A safe place you never want to leave.

CHAPTER EIGHT

A Good Egg

I could never in a million years have predicted that my child-hood New Kids on the Block obsession would one day in-tersect with my attempts to . . . freeze my eggs. Back then I had no idea that freezing your eggs was even a thing. I was more focused on Jordan Knight's dance moves than I was on my own future fertility. Have you ever seen him swivel and pop his hips? He was the next generation of Elvis, IMHO.

My sister Shonda and I were complete Blockheads growing up. If we heard "Step by Step" or "Please Don't Go Girl," it was ON. Growing up poor, we never saw the band live be-cause asking our parents for concert tickets just wouldn't have crossed our minds. We needed food to eat and running water, not boy band tickets. Being rockers, my parents didn't exactly appreciate boy bands, and even if they did, it's not like they would have saved up for months to get us tickets. I'm not bitter about it, it's just a fact. I think my first ever concert was Aerosmith and No Doubt, and I saved up for my own tickets out of my Dairy Queen paychecks.

When we weren't listening to NKOTB on our beloved boom box, Shonda and I would watch their videos on TV, and we would get so jealous of the kids who were at the live shows. We lived vicariously through them, imagining that one day, we might be there too. We had no idea that it would take twenty years for us to get that chance.

When I was doing *All My Children*, the band got back together and announced a reunion tour. Since I was on a soap and Shonda had become a businesswoman who owned her own spa, we had the means to finally get tickets. Shonda flew to New York, and we actually camped out all night long for the chance to see them perform on the *Today* show. I wanted to look cute because I thought this might be my shot to lock eyes with Jordan Knight and Donnie Wahlberg, like I'd long dreamed of doing. I decided to wear skintight jeans, which I quickly learned is a terrible choice when you're stuck outside on a New York City street for twelve hours with no bathroom, no chair, and no change of clothes. It didn't take long for me to regret my outfit.

The jeans were so uncomfortable that I actually started to feel sick, or maybe I felt sick because we basically stayed up all night on a Manhattan street in a crowd of people. Still, all that torture was worth it for the chance to see my childhood idols. As we waited on the street outside, a few people actually recognized me as Amanda from *All My Children*, so I ended up taking photos and bonding with other Blockheads that night, which was sweet, and it also helped pass the time and distract me from the vise grip that was my pants.

"Aren't you Amanda?" a few people asked as they walked by. "Why are you waiting out here in line? Can't you just get in without waiting on the street?"

Um, that was a good question, I guess.

I didn't even realize that because I was on an ABC show, I probably could have asked a publicist to get my sister and me tickets so we could skip the line and the overnight wait and slip through the velvet ropes. After that, the *All My Children* publicist set me straight about the proper ways to go about these things, and I've asked for passes since. I was so green and had never even dealt with a publicist in my life, so the thought of asking to just waltz right in never crossed my mind. I would have been better off, because have you ever seen cranberry sauce come straight out of a can, with deep rings all the way down? That's what my legs looked like when I took those jeans off after the show. I learned my first Hollywood lesson that day: get to the front of the velvet ropes when you can, and wear comfortable clothes.

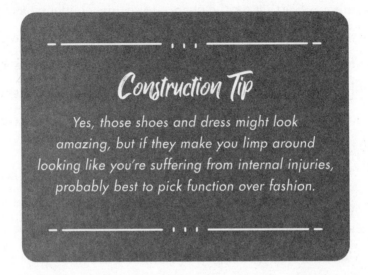

Construction Tip

Yes, those shoes and dress might look amazing, but if they make you limp around looking like you're suffering from internal injuries, probably best to pick function over fashion.

By the time security started letting people in to see the show, I didn't look as cute as I'd hoped. I was so exhausted that I had one eye open, and my jeans were so uncomfortable I felt like I was going to vomit. When NKOTB started playing, though, my inner preteen boy band lover came out, and I was that little girl in Kentucky again, freaking out over Jordan, Joey, Danny, Jonathan, and Donnie. I couldn't even feel my legs at that point. It was a dream come true.

Not long after that show, the band played a few songs during an episode of *The View*, and this time, I definitely asked for some VIP passes. I also opted for a cute fit-and-flare dress, because I was not about to make the same mistake again. I asked the hair and makeup team from *All My Children* to glam me up, and when the band came out to play, I was front and center. I'm sure there is footage of me dancing like a teenager that would embarrass most, but I'll always be a proud Blockhead. I was making up for all those years with the boom box, dreaming of being at a show. After they played, I got to go backstage and actually meet them. I tried to play it cool, but my heart was pounding and I broke out into a full body sweat. The hairstylist had curled my hair, but it was totally flat from sweat by the time I met Jordan Knight. He was very sweet, and I was self-conscious that he would feel me sweating when he put his arm around me for a photo. If he did, he didn't let on, but how could he not have? I was literally dripping. After our sweaty encounter, a huge security guard came up to me and said, "Donnie wants to meet Amanda." That was me! Or my character. Maybe he watched *All My Children*? Regardless, I was thrilled. I got to meet Donnie Wahlberg, which felt like the coolest thing that had ever happened to me. I saw the band in concert every chance I got after that, and then, in 2020, came another opportunity to showcase my love of NKOTB: *Dancing with the Stars*.

When I got the call about doing *Dancing with the Stars*, I was in an autopilot stage of life. In just a little over a year, I had lost both of my parents to cancer. I was in the middle of a divorce, and I had decided that, because I wanted a family and I was in my late thirties and suddenly single, I should go through the process of freezing my eggs. Each day was about putting one foot in front of the other, so when I was asked to do actual live choreography and learn how to rumba and waltz on television, the thought was terrifying. I'm not saying everyone needs to jump from sadness straight into salsa, but finding things to pull you out of sorrow or disappointment helps. My "thing" just happened to involve a glittery gold dress and Pink's song "Raise Your Glass."

I had already had to postpone freezing my eggs once, because of Covid. Clinics and nonessential surgeries were stopped because of the virus, and so the process kept getting pushed. When I got the call about the show, I was halfway through the daily shots for the round I had started, and so I decided that I could inject myself with hormones *and* learn to dance in competition. I hate needles, so stopping and negating all those shots wasn't an option. I did not want to go through it all again. Something I've learned about myself is that I'm usually up for a (terrifying) challenge. As I've mentioned, I was not and am not a great dancer, but this was a step up from potentially drowning on live television doing that show *Splash*. When I was doing *Dancing with the Stars*, I would rehearse with my partner, Gleb Savchenko, for about four or five hours a day, in addition to filming interviews and behind-the-scenes content. Every day, I would bring my hormone shots and store them in the refrigerator while we practiced. Since the medications all have to be administered at specific times, I would excuse myself and sneak into the bathroom to give myself the shots. One day, I walked out of the restroom holding a bunch of used syringes, and a security guard was standing right there. Once I saw his reaction, I quickly explained that it wasn't what it looked like and told him I was giving myself fertility shots. He was very understanding, so either I wasn't the first woman on *Dancing with the Stars* to freeze her eggs, or dealing with someone doing drugs in the bathroom wasn't part of his job description.

As hundreds of thousands of other women know, freezing your eggs can be extremely stressful. You go through a series of blood tests to check hormone levels, and then you're put on a course of shots to boost those levels so that the doctor has enough eggs to retrieve at the end of the cycle. It's not an easy procedure, because you want to get the most healthy eggs you can to have the best chances of having even one good embryo, and one chance at having a baby. And after all that, there are still no guarantees. I had helped a friend of mine with her first shots when she went through it, so I had a little bit of exposure to how it all works. Still, when you get a box full of strange medications with syringes and specific measurements and confusing instructions, it can be very overwhelming. Usually, if you're sick, you're at a doctor's office getting shots from a professional, and suddenly they're just trusting you to figure it all out. Once you get into the rhythm it's less intimidating, but it takes over your life in some ways. Add to that the fact that your stomach is all bruised from the injections, you start to feel uncomfortably bloated and tight, and all the hormones are affecting your mood and energy levels. At that same time, I was in escrow on two properties, so my life was still moving, and I had to keep up with it despite all the hats I was cramming onto my head. One couple I was working with was having a baby, and the other was selling their house, so I had to continue working for them and couldn't drop the ball. Needless to say, it was a challenge. When I look back at that time, I wonder how I pulled it all off, but as I was learning in dance, you just take things one step at a time. Even if you fall, and I definitely did fall, you can't get caught up in the outcome.

That first week on the show was definitely the hardest. I was learning the damn tango, a dance that's supposed to be erotic and fluid, and there I was feeling like I had a basketball in my stomach, which, at least for me, is definitely not a sexy feeling. I was on the show with people like Kaitlyn Bristowe from *The Bachelor*, Jesse Metcalfe, Nelly, Jeannie Mai, Skai Jackson, Anne Heche, Vernon Davis, *Catfish* host Nev Schulman, and of course, Carole Baskin from *Tiger King*. I went out of my way to be nice to her, because can you imagine if everyone was accusing you of killing your own husband? We didn't become super close, but she did follow me on Instagram. Probably best to stay on her good side anyway.

The steps I was learning to prepare for the show went against all my initial, two-left-feet impulses, so it took a while to get into the groove and feel the rhythm. If I was supposed to go right, I usually went left. Then there was the fact that "Raise Your Glass," even though I love it, is not a freaking tango song, so there were definitely some frustrating moments. I looked like I was having a live panic attack when we performed that dance, but we got through it. Let's be honest, I would probably suck at tango no matter what state I was in, so my hormone shots can hardly take the full blame for the fact that our scores were some of the lowest on the show that first night. We got two 4s, and I'm pretty sure Bruno gave us a sympathy point and threw us a 5. And yet, even though the only person to score lower than me that night was Carole Baskin, I didn't feel defeated. Gleb thought we were going to be kicked off, but I didn't. In a weird way, I'm very comfortable in the underdog position. People have underestimated me my whole life, so after we got our scores that night, I liked knowing that the only way to go from there was up.

Construction Tip

In real estate we like to say "underpromise, overdeliver." It applies to work, dating, or dancing. Keeping expectations realistic is key.

One of the highlights of the experience was when I saw that Donnie Wahlberg from NKOTB had tweeted that people should tune in to *Dancing with the Stars* the night we were dancing to their song "You Got It (The Right Stuff)" during '80s Night. The producers originally wanted me to dance to Madonna's "Like a Virgin," and even though I love that song I had no personal ties to it like I do to NKOTB, so I suggested that we pick one of their songs that had a cha-cha-esque beat. I was obviously already nervous, and that tweet just added a whole layer of excitement and terror. Would my childhood idols be judging me? Laughing at me when I attempted to pull off one of their signature moves?

Would they be performing? It turned out that they sent a personal video message to me, which made me FREAK OUT like the boy band fanatic I am. It was a huge confidence booster, so even though my cha-cha looked a little manic, it won over the crowd because I was genuinely having so much fun onstage, living my best fangirl life.

Long before I froze my eggs and danced a tango, I actually had my first experience of being a "mom." My own mom got pregnant with my baby sister, Sabrina, when I was fifteen going on sixteen, and when she first told me she was expecting a *fifth* baby, I was not happy. I told her we couldn't afford another baby, but as soon as Sabrina was born, I was in love. I was a teenager, but I quickly stepped into the role of mom, changing diapers, feeding her, putting her to bed. Girls and women tended to have babies pretty early in my small Kentucky town, but I still remember getting dirty looks from people who assumed I was a teen mom. Once in the laundromat, I was holding Sabrina when a woman scowled at me, as if I were some sort of horrible person for being a teen mom. Instead of explaining that she was my baby sister, I just leaned into it, saying, "There, there, Mommy is here," pissing the woman off even more. There was something in me that found it entertaining to piss off this judgy stranger when the reality of the situation was the opposite of what she thought: I was being a responsible daughter and doing laundry and watching my baby sister, with homework to do once I got home. Once Sabrina hit her twenties, I had to make a weird transition from pseudomom to sister/best friend. I am so protective of her even though she's all grown up now and has her own life, so I have to constantly remind myself that I am not actually her mom. When she talks to me about dating people I don't exactly approve of, I have to remain cool. Or try to.

Because I was taking care of a baby so young, I just didn't feel a burning desire to become a mom until much later, when I got married and wanted to start a family. I also knew that raising a child wasn't just about cute Instagram photos and adorable milestones. I had washed cloth diapers in a bathtub, so I had zero illusions about motherhood. As much as I'd like to say we were trying to save the planet by using the cloth diapers, it was just cheaper. Later on, I was so focused on my career that kids weren't part of my early vision boards. I didn't feel like I'd fully accomplished what I'd set out to do until I was on *Days of Our Lives*. There I was on another soap, proving that my first job on *All My Children* wasn't just a fluke. Having a family only started to feel realistic, and desirable, a few years later. I had a conversation about kids with Justin early on in our relationship because having a child eventually was important to me. When we got married, I became a stepmom and I loved fully embracing that role, but once we got divorced, my hopes of getting pregnant and raising a baby with a partner by the age of forty were quickly upended.

My mom never pressured me to have kids. She was always proud of my other accomplishments, and three of my other sisters had kids, so she wasn't relying on me to become a grandmother. One day when, hopefully, I do have a baby of my own, I'll be more regimented than my mom was, which will not be hard, but I also want to remember her free spirit and her sense of fun. If we dropped a piece of food on the ground, she didn't freak out about germs. She'd say, "God made dirt, so dirt don't hurt." She didn't panic about every little thing or follow us around monitoring our every move. As chaotic and difficult as my childhood sometimes was, it was also full of love, and nights when the whole family would dance to our parents' favorite rock songs together. Saying my mom wasn't a "helicopter mom" would be a massive understatement, but she did encourage us to be ourselves. She was more like the ultimate "free-range" mom, letting us go through life without many, or any, guardrails.

One thing about my parents that I really cherish is that they never told me my wildest dreams could not come true. My parents were creative and encouraged us in everything we set out to do, and that I will always remember. If I do have a child and they want to go into acting, I'll support them 100 percent if they're doing it because it's a passion. If they're doing it because they think it's cool or because they want money, I'll definitely suggest they try a steadier profession. I'm all for creativity and freedom, but I'm also practical. I've had to be.

I look up to the women in my office at the Oppenheim Group who are moms. Amanza is an amazing single mom who raises her kids alone, and she made it through a pandemic where she was sole provider and full-time homeschool teacher and a badass at all of it. We had real conversations about it, and it was not easy for her, but she did such a great job, and I take so much inspiration from her. I've taken her kids to dinner to give her a night off here and there, and I see how hard she works, but also how rewarding it all is. Mary is the same; she's so strong and she's constantly working so hard and she's such a great mom to her son. And with Maya, we joke that she's going to have a baby every season of *Selling Sunset*. I remember once when she flew across the country with a baby *and* her dog, and I was in awe. I can barely fly with my dog, it's so stressful. When I asked her about it, she said she has no idea how she did it either. Women get into that mode, and they just get shit done. That's why I love moms and women in general. I know so many women who are pros at multitasking and keeping things going, so I'm not going to let a divorce or age or anything else stop me. I'll figure it out. If it's something you truly want, you find a way.

I do have a major fear of having to raise a child by myself because I know how hard it can be and how much work it takes. So many women go through what I'm going through; they freeze their eggs or adopt and do it on their own. But there's also the guilt of feeling like you're a failure if you're not doing it the "traditional" way. We put so much pressure on ourselves. I know I did, and still do. Even with egg freezing, the goal was to get twelve eggs, and I only got seven because a cyst was blocking one ovary, and at first I took it personally, even though it was completely out of my control. I opened up about it all on *Dancing with the Stars* and on social media because I know other women deal with these things, and I also know how healing it is to have a supportive community. I loved hearing stories from other women. They reminded me that when things don't work out the way you want them to, you have to work with what you've got. So I have seven eggs instead of a full dozen. Now that filming has wrapped on season five of *Selling Sunset,* I may go in for more. I still have the tools and means to raise a great human being and have a loving family, whether that family is two people, three, or more. Because as they say, it only takes one good egg.

My Favorite Mom Advice

Do as I say, not as I do. A favorite of my mother's. Whether she was telling us not to smoke while smoking or instructing us to clean our room when hers was just as messy, this phrase was one of her favorites.

When you feel bad, put on music and start dancing. Dancing always makes things better. My mom wasn't exactly a bleeding heart if you went to her crying because something was wrong. And to her credit, as annoying as it was to hear this catchall solution as a child at times, it works. It's about picking yourself up and not wallowing. Always a good move.

Teenage girls are the worst. BUT one day they come back to you. Our mom told this to my sister Shonda so many times to help her through raising her own teenager. As a mom of five girls, my mother knew what she was talking about.

Sisters have to stick together. Friends and boys come and go, but sisters are forever. Growing up in a family of five girls, we had our share of fights. This specific lesson came in the form of literally tying us together with a rope or belt until we got along again. Again, maybe not the most modern parenting tactic, but it worked for us.

God doesn't make mistakes. My mom always taught us to love and accept everyone. She liked to remind us that the world would be a very lonely place if everyone were exactly the same.

I brought you into this world, and I can take you out. We never took this one seriously, which I am sure never helped my mom's cause in the moment, but she wasn't wrong. Also, give the woman a break. She had FIVE KIDS.

Just wait till your dad gets home. When she said this, we knew she meant business. If we didn't do some major damage control, we were screwed.

Learn to drive in the worst car, and you'll be the best driver. I learned to drive in the absolute crappiest, most run-down van ever. When I told my mom I should learn in a better, safer car, she told me that if I learned in the worst car, I would be the best driver. It's good advice for driving, and for life. In real estate, if you start out closing a deal on a house that's imperfect or flawed, you'll be much better at your job because you'll have faced challenges that will help you down the road. In a work environment, if you start out in the trenches, learning every aspect of the job, you'll one day be a better boss because you'll know how it all works, and what each person actually does. Basically, starting with the best of everything doesn't always yield the best results.

CHAPTER NINE

Dancing in the Dark

At my dad's memorial, my family made a rock music playlist that was the exact opposite of what you would imagine hearing at a funeral. Instead of silence or classical music or a somber organ, we played his favorite bands: Led Zeppelin, AC/DC, Def Leppard, and Guns N' Roses. Music was always a big part of our family, and it would become an important part of my healing through grief, but I wouldn't come to understand that until much later.

On the day of his memorial, we vetoed starched, uncomfortable black dresses and suits and all wore our favorite rock band T-shirt and jeans. It was a perfect tribute to his spirit, and to the things my dad loved the most. I think that the best way to deal with the toughest times in your life, which for me was losing both my parents, is to find a spark of levity or light in all the darkness. His memorial was a celebration of his life, and we found ways to laugh and bond through our tears. Here's a little bit of what I wrote for him after he passed away:

> I grew up in an unconventional family, and my dad was a drummer—the heartbeat of the music. Today we lost the heartbeat of our family, but I am happy knowing he took his music to heaven. It just got a lot more rock and roll up there.

My dad lived with lung cancer for four long years. He would always joke that the disease may have taken his long hair, but it didn't take his pride or his spirit. He was always such a rebel and a badass, and he dealt with his diagnosis the same way. He loved his five daughters and my mom, and losing him, while horribly painful, also bonded the six of us together. We knew the good and the bad, and we all came together for him.

Construction Tip

Grief doesn't just go away. It becomes a part of you. The trick is not letting it define you.

Unfortunately, cancer has become part of my story, and although we can heal and become stronger, the pain will never be erased. Anyone who has been through loss understands how it changes and affects you, but it doesn't have to define you in a negative sense. Like any disappointment in life, the key is to turn it into something that eventually makes you stronger, instead of letting it drag you down into bitterness and hopelessness. It's not easy to do, and of course, I sometimes still get hit with a wave of grief when something reminds me of my parents, but I can also look back at the good moments and appreciate those precious last few months or years we had together. I've been able to get to the point where memories make me laugh more than they make me break down, which I know is what they want for me. I wish we had more time together, of course, but the memories I do have, I treasure.

Cancer had to fight to take my dad down. He had more than one near-death experience before cancer ever entered the picture, and my mom and sisters and I had started to think my dad had nine lives. A few years before his diagnosis, he crossed the centerline and was hit head-on by a semitruck. The details of the accident were always a little vague, and my parents never told us the full story. It is truly a miracle that he lived through that accident. He spent weeks in the hospital and months in recovery. He got better, but he was in horrible pain and ended up getting hooked on the pain pills. He took so many that the lining of his stomach tore, and he was rushed into emergency surgery not once, but twice. Both times, we were told his chances of making it were slim, but he came out of it. The guy was almost superhuman.

I'll always remember him as that dark-haired, confident rock star drummer who loved to be onstage making music. It was shocking to me when I discovered, in my late thirties, that my dad had issues with reading. He was such a proud man, so it was apparently something he had always been ashamed of, and I had no idea until my mom told us he couldn't go to his doctor's appointments alone because he needed someone to help him fill out the forms. My dad lived a life where he was pulled out of school as a kid to help work and support the family through odd jobs, so he never got the chance to learn to read well. He went to a crappy, rural school, and school was never important to him anyway. Despite this, he still successfully raised five daughters, showed us so much love, and stayed strong until the very end.

There are so many cancer stories about people "fighting" and "battling" the disease, or doing amazing things like traveling the world or climbing Mount Everest before they die. Those stories are inspiring and they give people hope, but everyone handles their diagnosis in their own way. I have a friend who was diagnosed with leukemia, and he told me that he hated it when people called him a "warrior" or a "fighter." He said that some days he didn't feel that way, and he didn't always want to be strong. He was afraid if he admitted that, he'd be letting people down. My dad didn't go climb a mountain or travel the world, and after four years he was ready to go, and there is strength in that too. He told us he'd had a full life and that he loved us, and we got to say our goodbyes and feel closure when he passed away. We had four years to be by his side, which is why, when my mom was diagnosed and passed away just months later, it felt so jarring.

My parents were always so different from other people's parents. Their everyday clothes included my mom in her usual bell-sleeved shirt and bell-bottoms, and my dad, with his long hair, was in his favorite Led Zeppelin T-shirt. There were times when I was younger that I just wanted "normal" parents,

171

but as I got older, I got to a point where, instead of being embarrassed by their wackiness, I was able to embrace it and be entertained by it.

My mom was diagnosed in February 2020, and by July 2020, she was gone. Unlike my dad, she wasn't ready to go. She was scared and she still had so much life in her, so the two experiences, even though they happened back-to-back, could not have been more different. My mom was the kind of person where something was *always* ailing her. To hear her list her symptoms would be like listening to the end of a pharmaceutical commercial when they rattle off side effects. Because my mom always had a flair for the dramatic, I still feel guilty about the times we didn't take her seriously. For example, when she complained of back pain and we thought it was just another minor affliction, but she ended up needing surgery because two vertebrae were fused together.

For years I tried to help with any medications she was taking, and I knew all her doctors and had her pharmacy in my contacts just in case she forgot to refill a prescription. None of us had any idea how sick she was, and we were so focused on our dad that when she was diagnosed with terminal lung cancer, we were shocked. It was also during Covid, so at first I couldn't even fly out to see her. I was extra careful, and once I got tested and got the okay from the doctor, about three months after she was diagnosed, I flew to be by her side. Covid was bad enough, but sitting at home with nothing to do while you know your mom is dying of cancer was horrible. I know many people had it even worse during that time, but it was extremely painful to feel so helpless.

I don't know what I would have done without my mom during my divorce. She was right there when I needed her. The funny thing is my mom never even liked Justin. She'd never seen any of his shows, and she'd only watched a few episodes of *Selling Sunset*, so she just lived in a different world and was not won over by someone's celebrity. At the end of the day, she just cared about how someone treated her daughter. I'm not sure if she did it on purpose or as a dig, but she always called him Jacob. In fact, this little quirk ended up leading to our first big belly laugh as a family after she passed away. My sisters and I were all sitting together crying, and Sabrina asked me if Justin had reached out or not. I told her that he hadn't, and that I wasn't really expecting him to, but that it was okay because mom never liked Jacob anyway. So my mom kept us laughing, even after she was gone.

Because my mom was so unimpressed by celebrity or material things, her idea of the perfect day was relaxing by a lake next to a camper with a beer in hand. So when I was planning my second trip out to visit her after her diagnosis, I found an Airbnb cabin on a beautiful lake in Kentucky that would fit the whole family: my mom, me, and all four of my sisters, plus nieces, nephews, and brothers-in-law. I sent her photos of the cabin before the trip, and she was beyond excited. Part of my job is finding people their dream homes, and this one looked nothing like any that I had shown before, in the best way possible. It was in the middle of nowhere, and there was a slight mosquito problem, but it had lake views. To my mom, it was perfect.

During that trip, I had no idea that the next time I would see my mom—just a few weeks later—she would be in hospice in the hospital, unable to speak at all. But during that lake trip, we had one last, beautiful hurrah all together, going out on the boat, cooking, and laughing for the weekend. We gave her the primary suite, of course, and she was so energetic and happy. It's one of my favorite memories. While we're talking about my mom, one thing I should mention is that she would pocket anything and everything as long as it wasn't nailed down. She didn't steal, but if she thought something was free, she would take it. So for example, condiments at a fast-food place, peppermints at a doctor's office, or magazines in a waiting room. Once my mom left, the place would be wiped out. It used to embarrass me as a kid, even though I could never complain of a shortage of ketchup packets.

One of the things my mom would pocket was rocks. She

was completely obsessed with them. I remember catching her "collecting" rocks at our Airbnb by the lake and telling her, "Mom, those are decorations; you can't take those!" In the end, who really cares if she took a few rocks that a landscaper picked out? She was so excited by each one and was convinced that they meant something or that they had some amazing history. She was constantly telling us about a fossil she found or an extremely rare Native American arrowhead. Even though sometimes we had a hunch that the "fossil" she was showing us was nothing but gravel from the Patti's 1800's Settlement restaurant parking lot in Grand Rivers, Kentucky, we indulged her. It was a true passion, and even though we tried to explain that the actual parking lot was not from the 1800s, it made her so happy that we just went along with it.

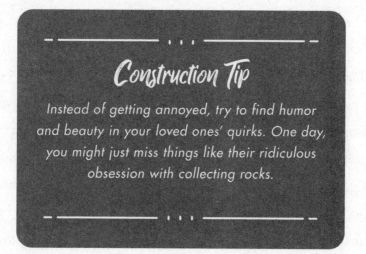

Construction Tip

Instead of getting annoyed, try to find humor and beauty in your loved ones' quirks. One day, you might just miss things like their ridiculous obsession with collecting rocks.

I'm not here to give advice about how to handle the pain and sadness of cancer, but I can share things that helped me, and that I learned. Like I've said, everyone handles it differently. I found that doing whatever you can to help keep that person's spirit intact, whether it's playing a certain song or joining them when they collect decorative rocks, helps both of you. Giving my mom something to look forward to was also important. We had that quality time, in a beautiful place, together. One thing I do know for certain is you cannot tackle it alone. Bring people in, have people around, and accept that it takes a village.

After our lake weekend, I was excited to plan more trips, since I knew the time with our mom was finite. She took a turn for the worse so soon after our trip, though, that another one would never happen. When she was moved to hospice, even the nurses were shocked at how fast she declined. I don't know what I would have done without my sisters, Shonda, Tabatha, Charissa, and Sabrina. Tabatha and I hadn't always seen eye to eye, but our dad's dying wish was that all his daughters get along, so we took that to heart. We worked out our differences. Losing our parents was the catalyst that brought us all closer together, as horrible as the experience was. We leaned on one another. We divided and conquered, because between the tears and sorrow, you have to sign paperwork and plan things and handle details that are not going to handle themselves. We started a family text chain that is still going strong; it's full of photos, inside jokes, and updates about everyday things that keep us connected. And lucky for me, my family understands my passion for speaking in Beyoncé GIFs, or if they don't, at least they humor me.

My sister Shonda and my brother-in-law Chris were in charge of creating a memorial spot for our mom's ashes. They planted a flowering dogwood tree in their yard and sur-rounded the trunk with her prized collection of rocks. Bor-dering that, we made a circle using beautiful, sparkly white rocks that she would have loved. It's exactly what she would have wanted, and exactly where she would have wanted to be, at my sister Shonda's house, the place where we all come together as a family.

Cancer is like a tornado that crashes into your life and up-ends everything. Once it strikes your life, it sucks the energy out of your work, your relationships, and your ability to func-tion in day-to-day life. It makes it hard to get out of bed in the morning or fall asleep at night. Being able to talk, vent, cry, scream, laugh, or commiserate with my sisters and friends got me through. A driving force behind my healing is know-ing that my parents would want me to be living a full, happy life, and that helps me stay positive. I know my mom would have been *pissed* if I hadn't done *Dancing with the Stars*, since she loved dancing so much. The night I got to dedicate a dance to my parents will remain the best memory I have from doing that show.

Normally stage jitters would hit me as soon as the voiceover said, "Dancing the contemporary, it's Chrishell Stause with her partner, Gleb." Instead, on that night, I felt my parents hug me and lift me up with pride. In that moment, I knew I couldn't miss a step if I tried. Scores had never been more irrelevant to me as they were during that dance, and I'm so grateful to the show for giving me an outlet to honor them in that way. After such a brutal year, the feeling of knowing I was exactly where I was supposed to be, doing exactly what I was supposed to be doing, was freeing. I danced to Grace Potter and the Nocturnals' "Stars," a song that I used to listen to when I was dealing with the darkest moments of loss. Suddenly, that night, the song transformed from the soundtrack of my grief to a beautiful tribute to my parents. They were right there with me, shining proudly, *up on Heaven's boulevard.*

CHAPTER TEN

Bringing It Home

I've traveled many different roads at this point in my life, from the gravel leading into a Kentucky campground to the winding drive to my hillside home in LA. The journey has been full of twists, turns, and unexpected detours and road-blocks, but looking back, I wouldn't change anything because it got me to where I am today.

Even when I dreamed big, I never imagined a house like the one I have now. It has European oak floors throughout, a chef's kitchen, unobstructed views of the canyon and the city, a heated pool and spa with a cabana and two outdoor firepits. My favorite thing about the home is that you can see straight through to the canyon as soon as you open the front door. I didn't even know those types of homes existed as a kid, to be honest. The ten-year-old or sixteen-year-old me would lose her mind if she saw the dream home I bought, or the luxury homes I show for a living. She would cry happy tears and jump up and down on the bed screaming. My version of a nice house back then, like I've said before, had two stories, no roaches, central AC, and a solid roof. There are a million sayings about the meaning of home, like it's where the heart is, or where you hang your hat. For me, through all the ups and downs of life so far, I've come to think that home is where you feel most like yourself. It's not about high-end finishes or the "right" zip code. It's a place that, more than any other place in the world, just feels *right*.

One thing I've learned along the way is that you can have the most gorgeous, perfect-in-every-way home, but it can feel like the emptiest place in the world if it's lacking the essentials: unconditional love and support. When I was married, I lived in a house that, on paper, was perfect. It was a sprawling, expertly designed modern farmhouse with all the luxury finishes, but looking back it wasn't truly my home. I didn't even end up taking much from that home when I moved into my own place after we split up. I took my clothes, my shoes, a few personal things like family photos, and Gracie, my dog. The only thing I forgot in my rush to leave was an Elvis print that I ended up going back for. (People either love the Elvis print or hate it, but no matter how elegant a room is, he'll always have a place in my home and heart.)

As hard as the move was after my divorce, the new place ended up feeling more like home than my previous house, because it allowed me to be myself. I did a lot of self-reflection and started an amazing new phase of my life there, while getting stronger each day. Changing out the heavy red velvet theater curtains the previous tenants had up was a must, unless you're into a *Rocky Horror Picture Show* vibe. Don't get me wrong; I love the movie, but I don't want to live in it.

Looking back on it now, that rental was actually the perfect transition house for me. I found it right away. It was furnished, had a great view (once you removed the red curtains), was located minutes from the office, and I could move in immediately. The landlord even came over with his wife when I moved in, and they brought over Whispering Angel rosé and amazing chocolates from a restaurant called Bottega Louie in downtown Los Angeles. What landlord does that? None that I had ever encountered. That was a "meant to be" moment. My life may have felt like a disaster, but I knew at least I had found the perfect postdivorce "safe house." It was what I needed to get back on my feet. I spent a year and a half in that place, and now that I just moved out and am finishing this book in my new home, I've never felt surer of the fact that everything happens for a reason.

When I lived with my grandma in middle school for one year, her modest house with plush carpet, a kitchen island (the first one I'd ever seen), and a finished basement was my idea of luxury real estate. It actually was a cute house—a traditional, rock-front home with a dirt driveway on about an acre of land. She had a cow that I would feed after school sometimes. When I left for college and lived in the crappiest little dorm you've ever seen, I was in heaven. It was probably about two hundred square feet, with two twin beds and a sink. We had a communal kitchen and bathroom, so it was crucial to remember your room key when you showered or you'd end up half naked in the hallway. As a bonus, one of my rooomates was always in a bad mood, but I was *happy*. I was on my own for the first time, working toward my dream and supporting myself, and that little dorm felt perfect. Well, except for that roommate. She would eat my food and was always mad about something. I think my upbeat nature got under her skin at first, but eventually it kind of calmed her down (or wore her down). I let it go, because I had things to do and plays to audition for. I was not going to let one sandwich-stealing roommate stop me.

Ironically, that roommate loved *Days of Our Lives*, and the first time I saw the show was when she was watching. It wasn't one of the shows my mom and grandma watched, so that's how I first got to know it. She would schedule her classes around it and always made sure she was free from noon to one p.m. to watch. I realized the only time I could be sure she was in a good mood was when we watched *Days* together. She would explain who all the characters were and gave me the backstories and drama. Little did I know, skipping class to watch soaps would end up being research for my future career. I ended up making the most of that shoebox dorm situation. Looking back, it was another place I was just supposed to be.

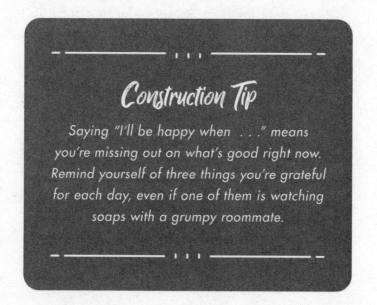

Construction Tip

Saying "I'll be happy when . . ." means you're missing out on what's good right now. Remind yourself of three things you're grateful for each day, even if one of them is watching soaps with a grumpy roommate.

Real Estate Lessons Learned on the Job

One question I am asked the most is from new Realtors seeking advice about starting their career. Starting out in real estate can be tough because it's expensive with all the fees and initial costs, and it can take a while to get rolling. This is why I always thought it makes for a great side hustle as you get established. It is flexible, which is great, but it also takes money to make money at first.

I once met a lovely fan who came by the office and was very excited to let me know she was taking her real estate test in a week, and that she had already put in her notice at the restaurant she was working in. I tried to explain to her that what you see on TV with *Selling Sunset* is a VERY condensed and glamorized glimpse into the actual work we have to put in to make that bell ring. Doing inspections and dealing with needing credits for plumbing issues aren't exactly the criteria for bingeworthy television, so you tend to see the fun stuff.

Here are a few things I learned on the job when the cameras weren't rolling.

Location is king. Always remember land appreciates and homes depreciate. So buy (and sell) accordingly.

First impressions are everything. Whether you are presenting a house for sale or a Realtor showing up for a listing appointment, you only have one shot to make a great first impression. Make it count.

Dress to impress. Something from the show that actually CAN help prepare you for the real estate workforce: dress to kill. Presentation, just like with the many homes you'll hopefully be trusted to sell, says a lot. Now are the sky-high stilettos necessary? Absolutely not. If I am not filming, I tend to be in much more reasonable footwear.

Keep an open mind. Just as in love, when buying a house, it is important to keep an open mind. Know your nonnegotiables, but try to be flexible about anything that isn't a dealbreaker.

Pick a lane. When working in real estate, like many fields, it helps to have a specialty to make you stand out. You can't know everything about everywhere, so pick a lane.

Learn from the best. Try to always surround yourself with people you can learn from. If you are the smartest person in the room, it will serve you well to switch rooms, especially in business.

Work smarter, not harder. Hustle and drive are very important, but making sure you are targeting your efforts for maximum payoff is important. Efficiency is key.

It's not about you. Focus on your client. Not the commission.

Don't get discouraged. Real estate is filled with ups and downs whether you're an investor or an agent. Play the long game.

I sell "dream" homes all the time, and if you've seen *Selling Sunset*, you know that some of these homes are ridiculously gorgeous: 180-degree views of Los Angeles, infinity pools (plural), marble countertops flown in from Italy, and giant movie screens that magically appear with the push of a button. If a forty-million-dollar home isn't filled with the right things, though, it'll feel more like an empty mall after-hours. A dream home should be about more than infinity pools and views, as nice as those things are. The real construction should first happen inside of you, and then you can get to the fun things like blinging out your closet or adding that light fixture you've been eyeing. I don't know if I would have found my Goldilocks, just-right-for-me home if I hadn't first gotten to a solid place in my life, after so much heartbreak and turmoil. I think my "just right" came just at the right time. Real estate is like dating. When it's meant to be, it'll happen, and you'll know. Of course, there's always the chance you'll get outbid or ghosted, but the key is to have a great Realtor and a positive attitude, no matter what.

As often happens in love, I had my heart set on another house entirely that, at the moment, I felt was THE ONE. Just like with men and marriage, though, everything happens for a reason. It was actually one of my listings, and I took the major step of writing a great offer, but I didn't get it because someone else came in with all cash, which in real estate usually wins the deal. When you think you find the one and it's not recipro-cated, of course there's heartbreak, but I have tried to stay in a take-it-as-it-comes state of mind and not wallow for too long. I still had my cozy rental, my friends, and Gracie. I thought that house was my soul mate, but life had other plans.

After that, I got "catfished" with one home that looked incredible online, but when I walked in, it turned out to be nothing like the photos. It was dilapidated and did not have a two-car garage as advertised, unless your two cars were a Smart car and a bicycle. It had an odd layout and felt a bit dark and sad, and the broken umbrella by the pool didn't help. Just like a guy who puts a hot photo from twenty years ago on his dating profile and then shows up looking like a different per-son, this house had not aged well. Jason talked me into looking at another home that day, and this one ended up giving me my Goldilocks, "this one is just right" moment. It had way better amenities than the house I THOUGHT I loved, it had incred-ible views, it was one level, and it had a private gate, driveway, and pool. Just based on the photos, I might not have gone to see this house on my own, but it turned out to be way better in person. When I looked at the pictures, I think I'd been so stuck on that first house, I wasn't even seeing it for what it was. After I walked through the home and fell in love, I put in an offer that very night. I can be extremely decisive when I feel like something is right. They had another offer on the house and they were about to counter, so I put my agent hat on and told them that if I came to them with their counteroffer that minute, we'd have a deal. And we did. Sometimes you have to apply the pressure to make your dreams come true. Nothing just falls in your lap.

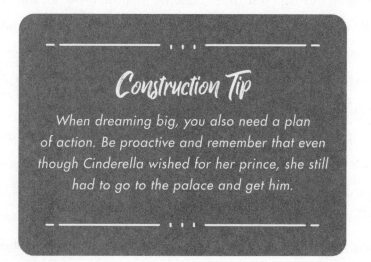

Construction Tip

When dreaming big, you also need a plan of action. Be proactive and remember that even though Cinderella wished for her prince, she still had to go to the palace and get him.

Moving into my home, a home I'd worked hard to earn (okay, fine, selling my wedding ring helped), was a major milestone that I won't forget. I'll never take the experience for granted, especially coming from my past. But it's not about getting the biggest or best home. Sometimes it's about doing a DIY reno on your apartment that makes you feel good, or doing some minor construction on your house that makes you feel proud.

When I walk into my home now (holy shit, it still blows me away that I'm a homeowner!), it's not too big or too small, not too showy or too simple. It's just right. For me.

It's a dream to have a place to call your own, and that place can come in many shapes and sizes. I've seen people with $50 million homes who are miserable, and my own family had some of our happiest times dancing in a trailer we all shared. Obviously we'd all probably rather dance in a $50 million home than in a shack, but still. You get the point. If the people in that mansion aren't making you feel good, then what's it really worth?

It took me a while to figure out what home meant to me: safety, love, coziness, and a place you won't get kicked out of at the drop of a text. In real estate, you make the most money when you do a reno yourself, when you put the sweat and work into a property before listing it. It's not always the easiest route, but often it's the most gratifying. At the beginning of my career, I was just happy not to be homeless, and not to be living in a run-down duplex that got shot up in a drive-by. I eventually wanted the American dream of marriage and kids, but sometimes with life you have to navigate unexpected turns in the road. The crazy thing is, I'm the happiest that I have ever been. Not because of a house, although I love my house (holy hell, I'm a homeowner, guys!), but because of the journey it took me to get there.

It's tough to get out of the cycle of renting, and it's tough to get a home. I spent my entire childhood acutely aware of this fact. The toughest part is the down payment, and I bought this place when I was just about to turn forty. I don't need to decorate it with chandeliers from Paris (although if you're offering one, I'll take it!). I'm all about mixing affordable things with higher-end pieces that you collect over time. On *Selling Sunset*, I'm often wearing a designer dress paired with off-brand shoes, or vice versa. Likewise, in my home, there's a beautiful view and pool, but the flowers are probably fake.

The thing I love most in homes are family photos. As a Realtor it's my job to tell sellers to hide their photos, but I love looking at them myself. They make a house feel like a home. I am not about the $1,200 pen holder that looks like an empty tin can save for the *Tiffany & Co.* engraved on the bottom. When you waste money on dumb things just because of a label, I feel like the company is just sitting back and laughing, like, *Look at this rich sucker who bought a tin can for a thousand bucks!* If that stuff matters to you, I'm not here to cramp your style. I just know that dollar amounts are not as important to me as mood, vibe, and warmth.

Selling Sunset is aspirational, and I would hope that it inspires and motivates people not to buy a mansion, but to reevaluate where they live, where they're at, and what they can do to renovate in realistic ways. Not everyone will attain the eight-thousand-square-foot palace on the hill, but I love when people share that the show inspired them to knock down a wall to let in more light. So even though our show is about the highest-end houses, it makes me happy that it can nudge anyone to update where they are, in the moment, in their own life. It's important to take the time to reevaluate yourself, your relationships, and your situation, and check in and ask what's working and what's not. What tweaks can be made to get the most out of where you are? Maybe a new door, or rearranging the furniture to help with the flow? Staying in a constant state of construction can actually be a good thing.

One of my favorite homes that I sold was not the most luxurious, at least on paper. I was working with a sweet couple who were expecting a baby, and we had a tight time frame to get them into a home before the woman gave birth. I found them a quiet and beautiful but unassuming home on a tree-lined street. Nothing flashy at all. The sellers had lived there for thirty years and raised their own children there, and I never would have guessed that my clients would have picked this home over the others I was showing them, but they fell head over heels in love. They had their Goldilocks moment. It was the sweetest thing, and they loved that it was meant for a family. It needed some work, but it was perfect for their needs, so signing up for the work was worth it.

As I have learned, life is one step forward and two (or, if you're a pigeon-toed dancer like me, maybe three) steps back. Life is about peaks and valleys and staying in a constant state of self-improvement. Whether it's great or terrible, it won't be that way forever. The highs and lows come and go, even though we hardly ever realize it in the moment.

Those vision boards I made in the early days of my career—pictures of awards, nice cars, and billboards—have changed. I'm still me (or as JLo would say, *I'm still Jenny from the block,* even though my block was a rural patch of grass in Kentucky), but my new vision board might have photos of a family, a kid, and maybe new career goals or a trip I'd love to take. It's more personal than it was before, but still very full of hopes and dreams. There's always construction to be done, goals to achieve, or life milestones to reach. I'll keep putting in the work, and never forget where the journey started: in a Kentucky campground, at the local Dairy Queen, in an abandoned schoolhouse with a faulty roof, but always with family by my side. I'm not sure where life will take me next, but I do know that after years of getting knocked down and pulling myself back up, I'm finally home.

Acknowledgments

This book was a labor of love that took many people to help it become more than an idea! First and foremost, I want to thank the beautiful writer Dina Gachman, whom I shared countless hours with and who through this intimate process I truly consider a friend. We bonded over the loss of our mothers and have shared so many laughs. You have championed this book and kept me on track when deadlines seemed overwhelming. You are so talented and dedicated, and every second of having the privilege to write with you has felt kismet and certainly meant to be. Thank you so much for your passion to help me tell my story. I've never written a book without you, and I happily never will.

Thank you so much to Brandi Bowles, my amazing agent at UTA who initially brought this opportunity my way and has worked so hard every step of the way to make sure every piece was in place.

ACKNOWLEDGMENTS

Natasha Simons is an actual angel, and I will never be convinced otherwise. I guess I watched too many movies, because my idea of editors, before working with you, was so off! I guess it makes for better on-screen drama, but you were never anything short of encouraging, endlessly helpful, and forgiving when I needed an extension. Thank you SO much for your care and expertise in helping me get to this page!

I am endlessly grateful to Simon & Schuster, Gallery Books, every single person who had a hand in putting this book together! THANK YOU, Maggie Loughran, Michelle Podberezniak, Mackenzie Hickey, John Seitzer, Jeb Brandon, Greg Harris, Aubrey Hale, and Carolyn Levin. Truly could not have done this without the help of all of you!

And finally I want to thank my friends and family. How many times did I call you asking for details of things I forgot, pictures, and advice? At the end of the day I want to make you proud, and I hope I did. I am so lucky to have you in my circle of support, and I would never want to do any of this without you. I love you all so much! If I lost everything tomorrow, I know I wouldn't lose you, and THAT makes this crazy journey so much fun.